AFFIRMING GOD'S IMAGE

Addressing the
Transgender Question
with Science and Scripture

J. ALAN BRANCH

AFFIRMING
GOD'S IMAGE

Addressing the Transgender Question
with Science and Scripture

J. ALAN BRANCH

LEXHAM PRESS

Affirming God's Image: Addressing the Transgender Question with Science and Scripture

Copyright 2019 J. Alan Branch

Lexham Press, 1313 Commercial St., Bellingham, WA 98225
LexhamPress.com

All Scripture quotations, unless otherwise indicated, are from the New American Standard Bible®. Copyright © 1960, 1962, 1963, 1968, 1971, 1972, 1973, 1975, 1977, 1995 by The Lockman Foundation. Used by permission. www.Lockman.org.

Scripture quotations marked NKJV are from the New King James Version®, Copyright © 1982 by Thomas Nelson. Used by permission. All rights reserved.

Scripture quotations marked ESV are from The Holy Bible, English Standard Version® (ESV®), copyright © 2001 by Crossway, a publishing ministry of Good News Publishers. Used by permission. All rights reserved.

Print ISBN 9781683592761
Digital ISBN 9781683592778

Lexham Editorial Team: Todd Hains, Jeffrey Reimer, and Erin Mangum
Cover Design: Brittany Schrock
Typesetting: ProjectLuz.com

CONTENTS

CONTENTS

ABBREVIATIONS

ASPS	American Society of Plastic Surgeons
BNST	bed nucleus of the stria terminalis
DSD	disorder of sexual development
DSM I–V	*Diagnostic and Statistical Manual of Mental Disorders I–V*
FtM	female to male
GID	gender identity disorder
GnRH	gonadotrophin-releasing hormone
GRS	gender reassignment surgery
INAH 3	interstitial nucleus of the anterior hypothalamus 3
MtF	male to female
VTE	venous thromboembolism
WPATH	World Professional Association for Transgender Health

ABBREVIATIONS

ACKNOWLEDGMENTS

I am grateful to the many friends and colleagues who have aided in the completion of this work. Chris Cornine has provided many insights regarding counseling and transgenderism that have been quite helpful. Blake Hearson and John Lee provided insightful comments and critiques regarding the central texts in question. Robert Matz offered numerous words of encouragement. Andy Holder and Jan Hudzicki kindly reviewed some chapters and offered helpful observations. Kenette Harder and her tireless staff at Midwestern's library found every article I needed, most of which are not normally found in a seminary library. Kenette is the model of professionalism and Christian grace. Harry Michael provided a wise sounding board, and I am blessed beyond measure by his friendship. I am especially thankful for Steve and Sherry Thompson, both of whom read the entire manuscript and made multiple editorial comments. I also appreciate Steve's gentle question each week, "How is that book coming?" All the final conclusions in the work are my own, and none of these friends or colleagues should be faulted for weaknesses in my presentation.

February 2, 2018

J. Alan Branch (John 10:10)
Kansas City, Missouri

INTRODUCTION

TRANSGENDERISM AND CHRISTIAN ETHICS

On April 24, 2015, Olympic gold medalist Bruce Jenner revealed he self-identifies as transgender. In an interview with Diane Sawyer on the television program 20/20, Jenner claimed God gave him "the soul of a female" and boldly asserted, "I am a woman."[1] On June 1, 2015, Jenner announced via Twitter that he is now "Caitlyn" Jenner and said, "I'm so happy after such a long struggle to be living my true self. Welcome to the world, Caitlyn. Can't wait for you to get to know her/me."[2] On the very same day as Jenner's Twitter announcement, *Vanity Fair* released its July 2015 edition with Bruce Jenner provocatively dressed as "Caitlyn" on the cover. Just a few weeks later, on July 15, 2015, Jenner received the Arthur Ashe Award at the ESPY Awards in Los Angeles. Wearing a white Versace gown, Jenner said in his acceptance speech, "I trained hard, I competed hard, and for that people respected me. But this transition has been harder on me than anything I could imagine, and that's the case for so many others, besides me. For that reason alone, trans people deserve something vital, they deserve your respect."[3] Jenner went on to advocate on behalf of transgendered children who are bullied and consider suicide. Jenner had facial feminization surgery, breast augmentation surgery, and had been taking female hormones for some time, and in 2017 underwent genital gender reassignment surgery.

Jenner's announcement is all the more stunning since he is remembered as the masculine, athletic man who won the decathlon at the 1976 Olympics in Montreal, setting a world record by amassing 8,616 points in the competition. His photo was famously emblazoned on Wheaties cereal boxes as he represented the "breakfast of champions." Jenner was the portrait for American virility and good looks, but his life began to take very strange turns. Divorced twice, in 1991 he married Kris Kardashian, the former wife of Robert Kardashian, one of O. J. Simpson's defense attorneys. Jenner and Kardashian became famous as their family was showcased on the reality TV show *Keeping Up with the Kardashians*, which debuted on October 14, 2007. The show seemed to have no other purpose than to promote the self-absorbed and narcissistic personalities of the Kardashians, with accompanying sexual immorality and lewd behavior. With this background in mind, it is hard not to see Jenner's announcement as part and parcel of someone who has leveraged nothing more than celebrity status into a revenue stream.

The case of Bruce Jenner/Caitlyn Jenner illustrates several key themes common in current transgender discussions:

1. Embracing transgender identity should be celebrated.

2. God is actually behind one's transgender identity.

3. People claim to have a female soul trapped in a male body, or a male soul trapped in a female body.

4. If you love children, you will agree with the avant-garde stance regarding transgenderism.

5. It is a noble and brave thing voluntarily to go through extensive surgery to transform one's gender appearance.

6. Such an experience is liberating.

Commenting on his own gender transition, Jenner said, "Bruce always had to tell a lie. He was always living that lie. Every day he always had a secret. From morning till night. Caitlyn doesn't have any secrets. ... I'm free."[4]

While Jenner may be the most famous transgender case in America, a virtual tidal wave of events has pushed transgenderism and issues associated with it to the forefront of our popular consciousness. On May 13, 2016, the Obama administration's Department of Justice and Department of Education issued a joint letter of guidance urging all schools to accommodate transgender students, including allowing them to use the bathroom they find most consistent with their gender identity.[5] In March 2016, the state of North Carolina passed a law that required people to use the public restrooms that corresponds with the sex on their birth certificates. In response, the NCAA decided not to allow any national basketball tournament games to be played in the state.[6] In February 2017, a Texas girl named Mack Beggs won the female state wrestling title, but she did so while taking male hormones as part of the process of transitioning to male. In my own community, students at a local high school recently chose as homecoming queen a boy who identifies as female. The list could go on, but events such as these and countless others have left many Christians confused and frustrated concerning how we as believers should respond to popular support for transgenderism.

In what follows, I will argue that transgenderism is not a trait like hair or skin color but is in fact an identity rooted in multiple causes and is completely inconsistent with Christian ethics. To demonstrate this thesis, I will begin by summarizing a brief history of transgenderism. In chapter 2 I will then discuss the vocabulary of transgenderism. In chapter 3 I will provide a biblical critique of transgenderism. In chapters 4 and 5 I will discuss various arguments often used to claim people are born transgender. In chapters 6 and 7 I will review the process of transitioning, including hormone therapy and gender reassignment surgery. In chapter 8 I will address transgenderism and the family, while in chapter 9 I will summarize my arguments and focus on the local church. My goal is to join conviction and compassion in an evaluation of transgenderism. Since the vast majority of us have never experienced gender dysphoria, it can be challenging to understand someone's subjective experience of this condition. We are called to show the love of Jesus Christ to the world, but how do we accomplish this when the culture is upending fundamental categories of gender? Love for the lost certainly means we should speak with mercy and kindness, but fidelity to God also means we must speak the truth, even if it is painful or unpopular.

This is a book for the church. My intended audience is sincere Christians seeking to understand the modern phenomenon of transgenderism. While I certainly hope to write persuasively to those outside the faith, my primary audience is those who follow Jesus as Lord but are confused by rapidly changing trends regarding gender identity.

I also need to add a word about language, names, and pronouns used in this book. First, I will refer to males who feel they are really females as MtF transgender, and females who feel they are really males as FtM transgender. The issue of which pronoun to use is a feisty matter for many people within the transgender community. In most cases, I will simply refer to each specific person by his or her last name. However, I will use the pronouns consistent with a person's natal sex. As we will see, these issues related to language are not minor but represent profound worldview debates.

Finally, a word to people experiencing gender confusion or parents of transgender children. I realize that much of what I say may not be what you want to hear right now. I do hope you will give a fair hearing to a traditional Christian stance regarding these matters. Before embracing transgenderism, it is at least prudent to investigate why Christian theology and ethics have consistently opposed the idea. Long-standing and deeply held ethical imperatives are only thrown away quickly to the harm of individuals who are rash in their moral reflection.

CHAPTER 1

THE HISTORY OF TRANSGENDERISM

Thomas Trace Beatie is the first "man" legally to give birth in the United States. Born in 1974 as the girl Tracy Lehuanani LaGondino, Beatie self-identified as transgender and, in 2002, started the process of transitioning from female to male. While Beatie began hormone treatments and had her breasts removed, she decided to keep her reproductive organs. This was followed by a legal change in status from female to "male" in the state of Hawaii. In 2003, Beatie married female body-builder Nancy Gillespie, who already had two biological children of her own but could have no more because of a hysterectomy. So the couple purchased sperm from an anonymous donor to have Beatie artificially inseminated, and Beatie subsequently gave birth to three children in succession. Thus, though Beatie is legally identified as a "male," she has given birth to three children. Beatie has since gone the next step and had surgery to modify her genitalia. Commenting on her decision to transition, Beatie said, "I never struggled with my identity, or fought it or tried to change the way I felt. It was just the simple fact of my existence: Outside I was a female, but inside I was a male."[1]

Previous generations may have been able to dismiss Beatie's actions as an odd occurrence, noteworthy only for its uniqueness. But stories about transgenderism multiply weekly, and what was once unheard of now seems omnipresent. Understanding the background to the modern transgender movement can bring clarity and perspective when developing a moral stance on the subject. Transgenderism has not emerged from nowhere, and in this chapter I will trace some of the significant events that have led to modern debates about gender. I will begin with some historical background of transgender-like behavior from the Roman Empire. Then I will discuss Magnus Hirschfeld, Harry Benjamin, the sexual revolution in the United States, and the influence of literary deconstruction in academic discussions about gender.

THE CULT OF CYBELE AND TRANSGENDER-LIKE BEHAVIOR

For us modern Christians it may feel at times as if no one else in church history has faced anything like transgenderism. But actually, the early church was familiar with something similar in the religion of Cybele, an ancient goddess-worship cult that had priests called "Galli" who presented themselves in ways similar to transgender people today. In ancient Rome, March 24 was known as the Day of Blood and was dedicated to Cybele worship. During a public procession, the high priest of Cybele would flagellate himself with a whip hung with knucklebones while marching through the streets. At the same time, men who wanted to become servants of Cybele worked themselves into a frenzy and slashed their testicles with a piece of broken glass or flint, castrating themselves in a painful fit of emotional hysteria while dancing. After castrating themselves, these Galli were attired in female garments, grew their hair long, and used perfumed ointments. They had their hair bleached and usually wore it dressed up and waved like women, a look completed by wearing heavy makeup, their faces resembling whitewashed walls.[2] As Robert Turcan of the Sorbonne says, "The galli consecrated themselves to Cybele by sacrificing their manhood to her."[3]

While the cult of Cybele has some striking similarities to modern MtF transgenderism, the parallels have limitations. It is not clear how many of the Galli emasculated themselves and cross-dressed merely out of misguided dedication to Cybele as opposed to men who may have experienced what today is clinically described as gender dysphoria. Thus, I refer to their behavior as "transgender-like" in order to acknowledge the differences. But while the motivations may diverge, the final behaviors are very similar. If we could travel back in time to early Christians in Rome in AD 64 and describe modern transgenderism to them, they probably would have said, "We don't have the word 'transgenderism,' but we think we have seen something very similar to what you are describing." Transgender-like behavior was not unheard of in the past, but how did modern transgenderism emerge in our culture?

MAGNUS HIRSCHFELD

If one person can be most credited for beginning the modern transgender movement, perhaps German physician Magnus Hirschfeld (1868–1935) is the best candidate. An advocate for sexual liberation from traditional values, in 1897 he founded the Scientific Humanitarian Committee, which was committed to arguing in favor of changing German law to decriminalize homosexual behavior as well as defending the rights of bisexuals and transgender people. To achieve these goals, Hirschfeld opened the Institute of Sexual Research in Berlin in 1919. On May 6, 1933, a little more than three months after Hitler became Reich Chancellor, the Institute for Sexual Science was ransacked, and much of its library went up in flames during Joseph Goebbels's infamous book-burning on May 10, 1933.

Much of Hirschfeld's activism was motivated by his own homosexuality. In 1919, at the age of fifty-two, he started living with nineteen-year-old Karl Geise and later added a second boyfriend, twenty-four-year-old Li Shiu Tong, whom he met while touring China in 1930. After the Nazis took over Germany, Hirschfeld took both men with him to France and claimed them both as lovers.[4]

Hirschfeld wrote during a transitional period in the conceptualization of sexuality and sexual ethics. It was during this time that many of today's sexual identity categories were initially constructed. Hirschfeld's rejection of traditional views of gender was foundational in the development of what is now called transgenderism. He said, "The human is not man *or* woman, but rather man *and* woman."[5] Most significantly, Hirschfeld's paradigm presented gender as existing on a continuum between male and female, with most people having characteristics of both. His work served the purpose of questioning traditional distinctions between the sexes and thus opened the door for future generations to embrace an ambivalent transgenderism. In his drive to expand gender categories, he once calculated there were 43,046,721 possible combinations of sexual characteristics, then indicated that the number was probably too small.[6]

In 1910, Hirschfeld published a monumental work titled *Die Transvestiten* (*The Transvestites*), in which he took the innovative step of distinguishing transvestites from homosexuals.

Hirschfeld himself coined the term "transvestite," which is Latin for "cross-dressing," and suggested that not all men who cross-dressed were actually homosexual, but their focus of pleasure was on themselves and their clothes. He also felt that women cross-dressers were more interested in the work roles and lifestyle of men than male clothing.[7]

Hirschfeld also coined the word "transsexual" in 1923. Distinguishing between transvestites and transsexuals, he described transsexualism as the adoption of the gender role opposite to a person's birth sex, arguing that such people hold an unswerving conviction that they are assigned to an incorrect sex. In contrast, he claimed that transvestites merely wanted to dress in the clothes of the other gender, but still identified with their natal sex.

Two of the first attempts at gender reassignment surgery were cases related to Hirschfeld's institute: Rudolf Richter and Einar Wegener. Richter (1891–1933) was a servant at the institute who preferred the female name Dora. Surgeons associated with the institute castrated Richter in 1922 and amputated his penis in 1931, and even attempted the daring move of giving Richter an artificial vagina.[8] Wegener (1882–1931) was a Dutch artist who married another artist, Gerda Gottlieb. On occasion his wife asked him to wear women's clothes so she could use him as a model. This experience purportedly awakened a desire in Wegener to become a woman, and he began to identify by the female name Lili Elbe. Eventually finding his way to Berlin, Wegener underwent five surgeries to transition to a woman, the last one an attempted uterus transplant. Sadly, Wegener died from complications related to this last surgery in 1931.

Hirschfeld initiated changes in thinking about gender and prepared the way for modern transgenderism in three ways. First, prior to Hirschfeld, transsexuals (equivalent to our modern term "transgender") were merely considered another form of homosexual, but Hirschfeld argued that transsexuals should be viewed as a separate and independent category. Second, he initiated the pattern of creating categories of sexual expression by inventing the words "transvestite" and "transsexual." Third, physicians at his clinic attempted the first genital surgeries to reassign a person's sex. While Hirschfeld set the stage for acceptance of transgenderism globally, another German physician was highly instrumental in changes in the United States.[9]

HARRY BENJAMIN

In American history, the most influential figure regarding transgenderism was German-American endocrinologist Harry Benjamin (1885–1986), widely acknowledged for his pioneering work in standards of care for transsexuals and considered the "founding father of contemporary western transsexualism."[10] He was an acquaintance of Magnus Hirschfeld, and their friendship helped direct Benjamin toward an interest in sexual matters. Transplanting to New York at the outbreak of World War I, Benjamin began treating transsexuals with hormones in 1948, when notorious sex researcher Alfred Kinsey referred a male who wanted to be a woman to Benjamin. While Benjamin did not provide gender reassignment surgery himself, he directed his patients to doctors who could.

In 1966, Benjamin published his groundbreaking book *The Transsexual Phenomenon*, in which he described his work with transsexuals and advocated a paradigm shift in their treatment.[11] He denoted three categories of cross-gender types: Heterosexual men who cross-dressed for reasons of sexual fetish, a second group of cross-dressers with deeper emotional disturbances, and a third type that represented a disturbance of the normal sexual and gender-role orientation.[12] This third group is what today we call transgender. Benjamin described this category by saying, "He lives only for the day when his 'female soul' is no longer being outraged by his male body, when he can function as a female—socially, legally, and sexually."[13] Benjamin forcefully argued that psychiatric attempts to change transsexuals were harmful and instead insisted that steps should be taken to help them identify with their subjective feelings of gender, saying, "Psychotherapy with the aim of curing transsexualism, so that the patient will accept himself as a man, it must be repeated here, is a useless undertaking with present available methods. The mind of the transsexual cannot be changed in its false gender orientation. All attempts to this effect have failed."[14]

Benjamin's most famous patient was Christine Jorgensen (1926–1989), born George Jorgensen. Jorgensen was a native of the Bronx and a US Army veteran. Between 1951 and 1952, Jorgensen had gender reassignment surgeries in Denmark performed by Paul Fogh-Anderson, one of the earliest surgeons to specialize in such procedures. On December 1, 1952, the *New York Daily News* blared the headline, "Ex-GI Becomes Blonde Beauty: Operations Transform Bronx Youth." Embracing the emerging arguments that people are born with a transgender identity, Jorgensen explained in a letter home to his parents, "Nature made a mistake which I have had corrected, and now I am your daughter."[15] Upon returning to America, Jorgensen became a patient of Benjamin's, and he assisted Jorgensen in finding physicians to offer further genital surgery. Jorgensen echoed Hirschfeld's ideas about gender fluidity and said, "You seem to assume every person is either a man or a woman. ... Each person is actually both in varying degrees. ... I am more of a woman than I am a man."[16]

Much as Jorgensen claimed "nature made a mistake," Benjamin argued that many of his patients were struggling with gender issues because of inborn traits that could not be changed and thus science and culture should help them adapt to their preferred gender. In 1984, he famously said:

> No true transsexual has ever been persuaded, bullied, drugged, analyzed, shamed, ridiculed, or electrically shocked into an acceptance of his or her physique. And so I ask myself, in mercy, or in common sense, if he cannot alter the conviction to fit the body, should he not, in certain circumstances, alter the body to fit the conviction?[17]

In 1979, transgender activists founded the Harry Benjamin International Gender Dysphoria Association in his honor, the world's first interdisciplinary professional organization dedicated to advocacy and treatment for transsexuals. The group later changed its name to the World Professional Association for Transgender Health (WPATH) and their standards of care for transgenderism have become widely accepted in professional communities.

THE SEXUAL REVOLUTION

That Benjamin's book *The Transsexual Phenomenon* was published in 1966 is no surprise. This was the era of the sexual revolution, in which Judeo-Christian sexual ethics were abandoned. In many ways, modern acceptance of transgenderism is the latest stage in the sexual revolution of the 1960s. Beginning in 1948 with Alfred Kinsey's *Sexual Behavior in the Human Male*, a concerted effort was made to discard biblical sexual ethics and embrace an avant-garde, sexually libertine ethic. The summer of 1967 in San Francisco was known as the "summer of love" for the hippie generation. By "love" they meant sex, anywhere and with anyone. Two years later in June 1969, the sexual revolution took another turn during the Stonewall riots in New York, widely accepted as the beginning of the gay rights movement. The Stonewall Inn was a somewhat dingy bar with Mafia connections located in Greenwich Village and long noted as a gathering place for transvestite prostitutes. When police made a vice raid on the bar in the early morning of June 28, 1969, the patrons rioted in a violent confrontation with police. The homosexuals and transvestites present that night were already agitated for two reasons: the bar had been raided a few days earlier on June 24 and Judy Garland's funeral had taken place a few hours earlier on June 27 in uptown New York.[18] But what should not be overlooked is the large number of transvestites who were involved in the melee. Issues of transgender identity were intricately related to the Stonewall riots.

While sexual promiscuity reigned in the sexual revolution, academia initiated the foundational idea of modern transgenderism: that sex and gender are two different entities. In *The Transsexual Phenomenon*, Harry Benjamin denied that sex and gender are synonyms, saying, "Gender is above, and sex below the belt."[19] This idea was articulated more fully in 1968 when Robert Stoller (1924–1991), a professor of psychiatry at UCLA, published *Sex and Gender: On the Development of Masculinity and Femininity*. Stoller also differentiated between sex and gender, saying:

> Gender is a term that has psychological or cultural rather than biological connotations. If the proper terms for sex are "male" and "female," the corresponding terms for gender are "masculine" and "feminine"; these latter may be quite independent of (biological) sex. Gender is the amount of masculinity or femininity found in a person, and, obviously, while there are mixtures of both in many humans, the normal male has a preponderance

of masculinity and the normal female a preponderance
of femininity.[20]

While the common consensus had been that the words "sex" and
"gender" were synonyms, Stoller divided the two terms, allowing
for new categories to be introduced into language. People now
talk regularly about the manner in which their "gender" differs
from their "sex," conversations that would have seemed confusing to previous generations.

The sexual revolution also targeted the family. Allen Ginsburg
(1926–1997) was a gay activist best known for his vulgar poem
Howl. His rejection of Christian sexual ethics entailed a redefinition of family, a point made clear when he said:

> We obviously are changing, altering in family struc-
> ture. ... I would see different kinds of family structure.
> Couple of girls with one guy, couple of guys with one girl,
> 20 girls, 20 guys, all making it if they want. Children held
> in common, matrilineal descent ... sharing.[21]

For the leaders of the sexual revolution, abandoning conservative
sexual ethics entailed the blurring of gender distinctions and the
redefinition of the family. In so doing, the sexual revolution of
the 1960s helped set the stage for acceptance of transgenderism
today. These radical transformations in sexual ethics were accel-
erated by changes in academia regarding theories of language.

LITERARY DECONSTRUCTION AND
CHANGING LANGUAGE

Literary deconstruction is an academic movement with origins
in the late 1960s and early 1970s that rejects authorial intent
as central to understanding texts and insists that no written
text contains a meaning within itself; instead, the reader brings

his or her own meaning to the text. Ronald Nash identifies the touchstone proposition of deconstruction as this: "It is impossible ever to know the meaning of any written text."[22] For literary deconstruction, language itself is an arbitrary, social construct that is often used as a tool of oppression. Borrowing some ideas from Marxist thought, deconstructionists argue the path to liberation and freedom is to throw off the constraints of language, particularly in relation to gender.

In our current context, an ever-widening array of gender identities is presented to us on a regular basis. Part of this confusion originates in literary deconstruction. Fresh! White, a Bay Area life coach and activist, and Holiday Simmons, who identifies as a black Cherokee transmasculine athlete, say, "We find ourselves frequently creating and changing the terminology that best fits or describes who we are."[23] These same authors go on to say they "use words that refer to the social construction of the gender binary, like 'Read as Female' and 'Female Assigned at Birth' because it makes it clear that these are descriptions forced upon me and they don't have any real standing."[24] Beyond feeling they had labels forced on them, White and Simmons enlarge the familiar LGBTQ acronym to an expanded LGBTT2QQAAIIP, which stands for "Lesbian, Gay, Bisexual, Transgender, Transsexual, Two-Spirit, Queer, Questioning, Asexual, Allies, Intersex, Intergender, and Pansexual."[25] By deconstructing language, transgender activists seek to change the way people think and talk about gender, and thus ostracize people who affirm the gender binary of male and female.

CHRISTIAN ETHICS AND THE CHANGING PLAYING FIELD

The sexual revolution ushered in a complete shift in sexual ethics. A cascade of events occurred very quickly that transformed the way people conceive of gender and sexual ethics. *The Transsexual Phenomenon* was published in 1966, the "Summer of Love" occurred in 1967, the Stonewall riots took place in 1969, and the American Psychiatric Association voted to stop describing homosexuality as a mental illness in 1973. The sexual revolution of the late 1960s saw Christian sexual ethics as repressive and the imposition of a false and constraining morality that impeded human freedom. The idea that Christian sexual ethics are oppressive and must be rejected is an idea that now pervades America.[26] Seen in this light, transgenderism is the ultimate rejection of Judeo-Christian sexual ethics.

Rejection of sexual restraint is intricately connected to philosophical debates about the use of language, particularly claims that language can be used as a tool of oppression. To a degree, Christians can agree that language can be used to oppress others. For example, when someone uses racial slurs to describe another human being, the slur serves as a way of dehumanizing another person, thus justifying exploitation or cruel behavior toward someone else. Likewise, when preborn humans are called "the product of conception" instead of a baby, pro-life Christians recognize language is being used to deny value to a tiny human life. In both cases—either using a racial slur or denying that the baby is human—a type of slander is occurring: The person using the offensive language is accusing someone else of something obviously untrue; that is, they are denying the image of God, which is coextensive with all of humanity. Colossians 3:8 comments on the ways language can harm others: "But now you also, put them all aside: anger, wrath, malice, slander, and abusive speech from your mouth." The phrase "abusive speech from your mouth" doesn't just have curse words in mind, but includes words we use to hurt others. Christians should use words that help and not harm others.[27]

The Christian worldview (in contrast to literary deconstruction) assumes that an intelligent God has created an objectively real universe that can be known, understood, and accurately described. Literary deconstruction is actually a radical form of skepticism that denies inherent meaning to the world in which we live, other than the meaning imposed on it by humans. In reality, the world is correctly and truly pictured by the biblical narrative of creation, fall, redemption, and the ultimate return of Jesus Christ. In this world (the world made by God and marred by a genuine fall), gender is an actual reality that can be described and embraced, along with the correct modes for gender expression corresponding to each person's sex. Because of the fall, people can embrace wrong ideas about gender. While some people may be born with a "disorder of sexual development" (DSD), which can cause ambiguous genitalia (I will address this later), there is no such thing as a man trapped in a woman's body or a woman trapped in a man's body: These concepts originate in misleading language games fostered by wrongheaded ideas rooted in deconstruction. There are only men and women, some of whom suffer confusing and frustrating ideas about gender because we live in a broken world. These people deserve our mercy. But mercy does not mean we affirm their linguistic charade. In the next chapter we will examine the expanding vocabulary of transgenderism and corresponding changes within the mental health profession.

KEY POINTS

1. Transgender-like behavior took place in the ancient cult of Cybele.

2. Magnus Hirschfeld and Harry Benjamin are fathers of the modern transgender movement.

3. Modern transgenderism emerged from the sexual revolution of the 1960s.

CHAPTER 2

THE VOCABULARY OF TRANSGENDERISM

I have a friend who is a successful team leader with a major corporation in the United States. He was quite surprised one day when he and all the other team members received an email from a female coworker announcing she is "gender nonbinary." Furthermore, she now wanted all other employees to refer to her only by her last name and to use the pronouns "they" or "their" when referring to her. The coworker acknowledged it would take time for other employees to accommodate themselves to her new identity. She closed by adding she was undergoing voice therapy and asked for patience as she learned to talk in a lower octave. My friend's introduction to his coworker's new identity was completed later that day when she entered the male restroom while he was washing his hands.

My friend's experience is common for many Christians today. New terms of gender self-identification seem to emerge overnight, leaving the uninformed feeling confused and bewildered. Where did such a confusing array of gender terms come from? In this chapter, I will begin by reviewing statistics concerning what percentage of people are transgender, then attempt to bring some clarity to the vast and expanding array of terms related to transgenderism, then discuss the transition in the way modern mental health professionals approach transgenderism, and finally review the influential case of David Reimer.

HOW MANY PEOPLE ARE TRANSGENDER?

Given the widespread visibility of transgenderism, exactly how many people can be called "transgender"? Estimates and data vary greatly and are affected by differences in methodology and variable definitions of who should be considered transgender.[1] In 1999, one group of researchers in Sweden estimated the prevalence of male-to-female transsexualism to be a wide range, between 1:12,000 and 1:40,000,[2] while a 2001 European study claimed a prevalence of 1:50,000.[3] In 2016, the Williams Institute at UCLA claimed 0.6 percent of, or 1.4 million, US adults self-identify as transgender.[4] In 2017, the Williams Institute also released a report that claimed 0.7 percent, or around 150,000, of youth ages thirteen to seventeen in the United States identify as transgender.[5] These reports can only give us an approximation, but the rising visibility of transgenderism means the church cannot pretend the phenomenon doesn't exist. If considered as a group, hundreds of thousands of transgender people worldwide need to hear the gospel.

DEFINING TERMS

The rapid appearance of transgenderism has brought with it a new and somewhat puzzling vocabulary. Just as missionaries need to learn the language of the culture to which they are ministering, it is important for Christians to understand the language of the transgender culture. Try to think of learning the language of transgenderism in the same way a missionary learns the language of a people group to be evangelized. It is impossible to communicate the gospel to a nation unless you know their language. Likewise, people in the transgender community have their own language, terms, and definitions that they use in daily speech. Learning transgender language does not mean we embrace their worldview, but it does mean we try very hard to understand them.

When the issue is transgenderism, many Christians may immediately have what pastor Vaughan Roberts calls a "yuk" response, as in, "Yuk, that's disgusting."[6] Indeed, a conscience that has been shaped by the word of God and an intimate walk with Christ will be burdened when addressing extreme deviation from biblical standards, but reaching people requires us to learn what they mean when they use certain terms in order to engage them with the gospel. Let's start with a brief review of transgender vocabulary.

Sex and Gender

Prior to defining "transgenderism," we must explain the main presupposition of modern transgender discussions: sex and gender are separate, identifiable concepts. As we saw in chapter 1, both Harry Benjamin and Robert Stoller severed these terms from each other in the 1960s. Still, for most people, the words "sex" and "gender" are synonyms, but in modern transgender discussions they mean very different things. "Sex" is used in reference to biological and anatomical traits such as obvious differences between genitalia, bone structure, DNA, hormones, and internal reproductive anatomy. In contrast, gender is used to describe the subjective psychological, social, and cultural aspects of being male or female.[7] To be clear, from a secular perspective, gender is a *feeling-based* concept and is disconnected from biology. To keep the differences clear, authors often refer to a person's sex as "male" or "female" and gender as "masculine" or "feminine."

Two related terms are "gender identity" and "gender role." Gender identity is also a feeling-based concept concerning how one psychologically perceives oneself as either masculine or feminine. "Gender role" can be defined as "the overt behavior one displays in society, the role which he plays, especially with other people, to establish his position with them insofar as his and their evaluation of gender is concerned."[8] While these terms can be confusing, this means a person could identify subjectively as a male while playing the role of a female. The categories of "gender identity" and "gender role" are used to reinforce the central tenet of transgenderism: sex and gender are separate, identifiable concepts, and there is no guarantee that one's gender identity will be consistent with one's biological sex. This crucial distinction between sex and gender sets the stage for the definition of "transgender."

Transgender

The American Psychological Association defines "transgender" as follows: "Transgender is an umbrella term for persons whose gender identity, gender expression, or behavior does not conform to that typically associated with the sex to which they were assigned at birth."[9] Transgender is an overarching term that describes and unites a broad category of people for whom their current gender identity is different from what is commonly expected of their birth sex.[10] In other words, their body is one *sex* (male or female), while they identify as the opposite *gender* (masculine or feminine). There are many different subcategories under transgender, including transsexual, transvestite, gender-variant, gender fluid, genderqueer, and cross-dresser. Often these terms overlap and are difficult to distinguish.[11] We should also add that transgenderism is different from sexual orientation, which refers to a person's sexual identity concerning the gender of the person to whom they are attracted.

Transsexual

"Transgender" and "transsexual" are often used as synonyms, but there are some differences. A transsexual is a transgender person who believes he or she was born in the "wrong body" and transitions via medical interventions to the opposite gender. A transgender person who is transsexual may be born with the genitalia of a boy, but considers himself to be a girl, or may be born with the genitalia of a girl, but consider herself to be a boy. All transsexual people are transgender, but not all transgender people are transsexual.[12] Again, the terms are often used as synonyms. When a person who is born male transitions to a female, he is called a "trans-female" or "male-to-female" (MtF). When a person who is born female transitions to male, she is called a "trans-male" or "female-to-male" (FtM).

Transvestites

Transvestites have a preference for cross-dressing but have no desire to pursue sexual reassignment surgery, and may simply be called cross-dressers.[13] Frequently, transvestite cross-dressing is fetishistic; the cross-dressing is associated with sexual arousal, but in such cases it usually does not imply the person wants to transition or even self-identifies as transgender. An important distinction needs to be made here: Many transgender people do not cross-dress primarily for the purpose of sexual gratification, but do so out of confused feelings of gender dysphoria. In contrast, a transvestite cross-dresses because doing so specifically leads to sexual arousal.

Two qualifications need to be added here. First, while people experiencing gender dysphoria may not cross-dress for the sole purpose of sexual gratification, they usually have a desire to play the role of the opposite sex in intercourse. Second, there are cases in which what begins as fetishistic transvestitism, especially in men, moves over time to transgenderism and a desire to transition to the other sex.[14]

Cisgender and Gender Binary

Transgender activists frequently use the term "cisgender" to refer to people who are not transgender. Cisgender means there is a match between a person's birth sex and the gender they feel themselves to be. Cisgender is not entirely a morally neutral term: Transgender activists prefer this newly created word because they claim the traditional terms "natural," biological," or "genetic" males and females assume the normalcy of feeling and acting in accordance with one's birth sex, thus making a moral judgment on transgender people.[15] The word "cisgender" was coined in the 1990s by German professor Volkmar Sigusch, who argued for "dismantling the old patterns of sexuality and reassembling them anew."[16]

When the term "cisgender" is used, it is often joined with the term "gender binary," which some transgender activists use as a derisive way of referring to people who divide the human race into two genders. "Cisgender" and "gender binary" often serve as shorthand for the Judeo-Christian moral tradition. As we will see later, Scripture affirms the binary gender expression of male and female: people are one or the other, and androgyny is not an option. Because many transgender advocates want to blur gender distinctions, hostile opposition to the gender binary as articulated by Christianity is central to transgenderism.

Disorders of Sexual Development and Intersex

Sometimes children are born with rare conditions in which their genitals are somewhat ambiguous, not clearly identifiable as male or female. Such children have a "disorder of sexual development" (DSD), a term referring to a number of identifiable genetic or biological anomalies that can lead to a failure of the genitals to develop in a normal fashion. In recent years, the term "intersex" has been adopted by many people born with such a condition. Children with a DSD are often leveraged in moral arguments in favor of transgenderism to say there is no gender binary but that gender exists across a spectrum.

Neutrois, Agender, Bigender

In an effort to circumvent the gender binary, other terms used include "neutrois," "agender," and "bigender." Neutrois refers to a person who is neutral; that means they are neither male nor female in gender. Sometimes the word "agender" is used as a synonym for "neutrois." Other people even self-identify as bigender, meaning they claim a dual-gender identity, with two sides expressed either simultaneously or at different times.[17]

Genderqueer, Gender Fluid, and Gender Expansive

The word "queer" was in the past used as an extremely negative epithet and slur in reference to homosexuals, but the word has been embraced by extremely progressive sexual revolutionaries who want to deconstruct gender and sexual moral traditions. The newly invented academic discipline of queer theory has embraced the task of dismantling normative categories of identity related to gender and sexuality.[18] For others, identifying as queer isn't meant to define the person's gender identity or sexual orientation, but is intended to let others know that the person identifies somewhere in the LGBTQ community.[19]

A specific term within queer theory is "genderqueer," which the American Psychological Association defines as follows:

> Genderqueer is a term that some people use who identify their gender as falling outside the binary constructs of "male" and "female." They may define their gender as falling somewhere on a continuum between male and female, or they may define it as wholly different from these terms. They may also request that pronouns be used that are neither masculine nor feminine, such as "zie" instead of "he" or "she," or "hir" instead of "his" or "her." Some genderqueer people do not identify as transgender.[20]

Others have defined "genderqueer" as an umbrella term for "people who do not identify exclusively as a man or a woman, or as something outside those two concepts."[21]

Often, genderqueer is used as synonym with "nonbinary" or "gender fluid," meaning a person rejects the exclusive categories of either male or female. "Gender fluid" means a person alternates between male and female or other various positions on a continuum between male and female.[22] In other words, such a person may identify as male on one day, female the next, and somewhere in between the day after. A related term is "gender expansive," a phrase developed by the Human Rights Campaign in 2012 to describe youth who did not identify with traditional gender roles but were otherwise not confined to one gender narrative or experience.[23]

Genderist / Transphobia

Transgender activists have also invented terms to describe people who are uncomfortable with transgenderism. The term "genderist" is used similarly to the term "racist." Developmental psychologist Diane Ehrensaft says, "The term genderist has evolved to describe a set of beliefs and practices that derive from the assumption that there are only two genders and that those who stray from their assigned gender boxes, male or female, are to be challenged, chastised, or cajoled toward normativity."[24] Similarly, transgender activists claim people guilty of transphobia have an irrational fear of transgender people based on prejudices and bigotry. Quite often, Christianity is blamed as the source of such bigotry.

Gender Dysphoria

The American Psychiatric Association defines "gender dysphoria" as the clinical diagnosis for the experience of distress among people who have a marked incongruence between the gender they were assigned at birth and their experienced or expressed gender, and these feelings persist for at least six months' duration.[25] In gender dysphoria, one's psychological and emotional gender identity does not match one's biological sex, and this leads to mental health problems.[26] It should be emphasized that one can only be diagnosed with gender dysphoria if he or she expresses significant distress or problems functioning related to the gender conflict. Thus, from a clinical perspective, not all transgender people are necessarily suffering from gender dysphoria. What this means is that if a person experiences the sense of being "a woman trapped in a man's body" but is not disturbed by this and it does not impair his daily functioning, then he does not qualify for being diagnosed with gender dysphoria. In informal conversation, gender dysphoria is sometimes used in a nontechnical way as a synonym for transgenderism. The term "gender dysphoria" is of somewhat recent origin as a clinical diagnosis, and the story of its development underscores some changes in perspectives within psychiatry and psychology regarding transgenderism.

MODERN MENTAL HEALTH PROFESSIONS AND TRANSGENDERISM

The expanding category of gender terms has coincided with identifiable shifts in the *Diagnostic and Statistical Manual of Mental Disorders* (*DSM*), now in its fifth edition. The trajectory over the last fifty years has been to normalize transgender behavior. Published by the American Psychiatric Association, the *DSM* is a classification of mental disorders with associated criteria designed to help mental health professionals make more accurate diagnoses, and it serves as an important point of reference in both clinical practice and academic discussions.

The various versions of the *DSM* reflect changes in the way modern psychiatry views transgenderism. In 1952, the *DSM I* called both homosexuality and transvestitism "sexual deviancy."[27] The *DSM II* in 1968 also referred to "sexual deviations," including homosexuality and transvestitism. Reflecting concepts at least similar to the Christian worldview, sexual deviancy was defined as "individuals whose sexual interests are directed primarily toward objects other than people of the opposite sex."[28] After intense lobbying and pressure from radical gay rights groups in the early 1970s, homosexuality was removed as a mental disorder, and the revised seventh printing of the *DSM II* in 1974 only mentioned "sexual orientation disturbance," a category for homosexuals distressed by their desires for same-sex intercourse.[29]

The *DSM III*, published in 1980, was the first edition to mention disorders specifically related to changing concepts of gender. Under the class of "psychosexual disorders" was listed the new diagnosis of "gender identity disorder," which was defined as "an incongruence between anatomic sex and gender identity."[30] Transsexualism was first introduced in the *DSM III* as a subset of gender identity disorder, defined at that time as a "persistent wish to be rid of one's genitals and to live as a member of the other sex."[31]

The *DSM IV* was released in 1994 and also referred to gender identity disorder, commenting that people with this diagnosis "are preoccupied with their wish to live as a member of the other sex."[32] The *DSM IV* also mentioned "transvestic fetishism," which basically referred to men who cross-dressed for reasons related to sexual arousal.[33] In 2013, the diagnosis of gender identity disorder was dropped in the *DSM V* in favor of the new diagnosis of gender dysphoria, defined as a "marked incongruence between one's experienced / expressed gender and assigned gender, of at least 6 months' duration."[34] At least part of the reason for the shift away from the diagnosis of gender identity disorder to gender dysphoria is that gender dysphoria is considered a less stigmatizing term.[35] Reflecting the development of new gender categories, the *DSM V* also mentions desires for "alternative gender identities beyond binary stereotypes."[36] In other words, the American Psychiatric Association no longer feels bound by the simple categories of "male" and "female."

What should not be missed is the manner in which the categories regarding gender shifted over the several decades within the American Psychiatric Association. Early versions of the *DSM* assumed the normalcy of opposite-sex attraction and identity with one's own gender. The categories of "deviancy" assumed that heterosexuality was normal and anything else was not, a stance that assumed a moral worldview at least echoing Judeo-Christian ethics. But after the sexual revolution of the late 1960s, the *DSM* quickly adopted the spirit of the age and normalized categories of sexual behavior the Bible clearly calls sin.

What many Christians will find frustrating is the degree to which the sections within the *DSM* regarding sex and gender seem so very different from other sections. Christians with some experience with depression or drug addiction will find the chapters in the *DSM* on these topics to be sound. But the same careful and crisp thinking reflected in these chapters on depression and addictions seems to be abandoned in discussions of sex and gender. At times, politically driven sexual agendas seem to replace a concern for best practice.[37]

Previous generations of mental health professionals sought to help people with what is now called gender dysphoria by directing them toward acceptance of their own body, seeing the ultimate goal as embracing the gender that corresponds to one's body. A minority of professionals still see this as the best approach. But the majority within modern psychiatry and psychology suggest that multiple outcomes may be viable. Some patients may learn to cope with their gender dysphoria by accepting their body; others may choose to cross-dress occasionally or permanently without medical transition; and yet others may have gender reassignment surgeries. Overall, the American Psychiatric Association has moved further and further away from any negative opinions about transgenderism, and in this way its stance on transgenderism is following the same trajectory as its stance on homosexuality. As transgender activist Nicholas Teich says, "It took until 1973 to rid the DSM of a diagnosis of homosexuality as a mental health disorder, so transgenderism may be following that course, just several decades behind."[38]

Beyond the American Psychiatric Association, the American Psychological Association also does not see transgenderism as a mental health disorder, saying, "A psychological state is considered a mental disorder only if it causes significant distress or disability. Many transgender people do not experience their gender as distressing or disabling, which implies that identifying as transgender does not constitute a mental disorder."[39]

From the perspective of many modern mental health professionals, if transgender people do experience stress and anxiety,
transgenderism itself isn't the cause of negative mental health
outcomes. Rather, these problems are associated with the stress
of living in a social environment that is not friendly to transgenderism. Usually this negative environment is attributed to
people affirming a Judeo-Christian worldview. In other words,
Christian disapproval of transgenderism is the cause of negative
mental health outcomes often associated with transgenderism.

There is little sympathy for Christian mental health professionals who might reject certain aspects of transgenderism. A 2013 report by the British Royal College of Psychiatrists
affirmed transgenderism and said, "Religious beliefs or cultural
mores must not be used to withhold, withdraw, or denigrate
treatment."[40] Likewise, the American Psychological Association
emphasizes that counselors should not stigmatize transgenderism, saying:

> Psychologists may model an acceptance of ambiguity
> as [transgender] people develop and explore aspects of
> their gender, especially in childhood and adolescence. A
> nonjudgmental stance toward gender nonconformity can
> help to counteract the pervasive stigma faced by many
> [transgender] people and provide a safe environment to
> explore gender identity and make informed decisions
> about gender expression.[41]

The American Counseling Association also says competent
counselors will affirm a person so they can experience a fully
functioning and emotionally healthy life "while embracing the
full spectrum of gender identity expression, gender presentation, and gender diversity beyond the male-female binary."[42] This
approach makes the moral judgment that transgenderism should

be embraced and assumes that a negative moral evaluation is discriminatory toward people experiencing gender dysphoria.

A common theme in pro-transgender literature is that there are no or very few demonstrable, successful conversions of transgender people via counseling alone, and thus gender reassignment surgery (GRS) seems to be the preferred method of treatment of gender dysphoria. Gennaro Selvaggi and James Bellringer, two European plastic surgeons specializing in GRS, justify their surgeries based on poor outcomes of therapy and go so far as to say, "Most professionals concur that gender reassignment surgery, or 'adjusting the body to the mind,' is the best way to assist individuals with severe gender dysphoria who desire this procedure."[43]

THE TRAGIC CASE OF DAVID REIMER

One of the most tragic and often-cited stories in discussions regarding transgenderism is the case of David Reimer (1965–2004). At age seven months, Reimer's penis was accidently mutilated in a botched circumcision. Uncertain what to do and terribly traumatized at their son's accident, David's parents were soon put in touch with John Money (1921–2006), a Johns Hopkins psychologist and sex expert. Money advised the parents to have David castrated and raised as a girl, which they did, calling him "Brenda."[44] In 1972, Money offered positive reports of the child's progress, saying the child enjoyed wearing dresses and that "she loves to have her hair set."[45]

Money's glowing reports of successfully raising a mutilated boy as a girl proved to be inaccurate and misleading. In 1997, Milton Diamond and Keith Sigmundson reported in the *Archives of Pediatrics and Adolescent Medicine* that David had rejected a female identity and returned to living as a male. David's mother told these researchers that as a child David would rip off dresses and, even though his parents encouraged him to play with girl's toys, continued to prefer guns and trucks to dolls. Teasing from other children was a constant problem because he looked like a girl but had the mannerisms and attributes of a boy. At age fourteen, he decided to begin living as a male, and at that time his parents revealed to him what had happened as a child. Eventually, he had surgery to make his genitalia look more masculine, and at age twenty-five he married a woman.[46] Reimer's life ended in tragedy when he committed suicide in 2004.

Many aspects of Money's therapy were morally repulsive, leaving one to question what, if any, moral center existed within him. Reimer and his twin brother made annual pilgrimages from their Canadian home to see Money at Johns Hopkins Hospital, where Money would counsel both boys together. Money brought a transsexual to demonstrate to David how a man can become a woman. His disturbing advice went so far as to encourage both Ron and Janet Reimer to let David see both parents naked in order for the child to learn the difference in sex organs.[47] Without the parents' knowledge, Money showed pornography to the twins in counseling. Perhaps the most vile thing Money did was to make young David (as Brenda) and his twin brother Brian mimic sexual acts with each other, something he forced the children to do at *age six*, going so far as to take photographs of the children.[48] Both children were deeply traumatized by this abuse.

The tragic case of David Reimer is often cited in transgender arguments, with the frequent claim that his experience is analogous to modern transgender people. Psychoanalyst Patricia Gherovici says, "This case study has become the most powerful example supporting the hypothesis of an innate gender identity."[49] In other words, they claim Reimer's case proves one can have a subjective gender identity that differs from how the person's body appears. David Reimer was told he was a girl, but deep on the inside he knew he was a boy. Likewise, transgender people assert a similar experience: They have been told they are one gender and raised according to that gender, but deep on the inside they feel they are the opposite gender, regardless of the body's appearance. When David Reimer's parents and physicians refused to accept his true gender, he suffered unspeakable pain that contributed to his suicide later in life.

Similarly, modern transgender activists claim that when a transgender child is forced to "live a lie" as the wrong gender, it leads to repressed pain and internalized hatred that can lead to suicide or other forms of self-harm. Since everyone wants children to be loved, nurtured in a loving home, and not to commit suicide, the David Reimer case is used as evidence that denying a child's true inner gender identity is harmful and destructive, and trying to force them to adopt a gender that is inconsistent with the child's own self-understanding will be as unsuccessful as the tragic case of David Reimer.

When all of the variables related to the David Reimer case are considered, we must question the degree to which his experience is parallel to that of people who self-identify as transgender. David Reimer was born a boy. Sadly, he was a boy who experienced a horrendous accident at a young age, the consequences of which were compounded when he came under the misguided care of John Money. People claiming a transgender identity in our culture do not have either of these shared experiences. Instead, they have normal bodies that function perfectly and have not been damaged, but they claim their subjective feelings do not match their undamaged bodies. David Reimer's feelings did not match what people told him because his body had been damaged by inept surgery and his soul had been damaged by ludicrous attempts at psychological experimentation.

SUMMARY

The vocabulary of transgenderism won't remain stable but will continue to change as different sexualities are mainstreamed. Many young people are rejecting these labels altogether and are embracing a broad, permissive, and promiscuous view of sex and gender. For example, one teenage girl responded to the question of sexual identity by saying, "I like what I like regardless of what's down their pants. If someone's attractive, they're attractive. The end. No identity."[50] As this young lady's sexual anarchy suggests, even as definitions are offered, they will change and transform over time. The ever-expanding glossary of gender terms allows an infinite variety of options for expression and identity. An effective missionary always stays abreast of changes within the people group with whom he or she is sharing the gospel.

Modern mental health theory argues that the healthiest manner of treating gender dysphoria is to embrace one's own subjective feelings, reject any notion that the sex of one's body determines one's gender, and pursue the process of transitioning. Mental health professionals who suggest otherwise are frequently ostracized and castigated. How do we as Christians evaluate these enormous cultural shifts? The answer begins with a firm understanding of gender from a biblical perspective, which we will examine in the next chapter.

KEY POINTS

1. "Transgender" is an umbrella term for persons whose gender identity, gender expression, or behavior does not conform to that typically associated with the sex they were assigned at birth. There are many subcategories of transgenderism.

2. Gender dysphoria is the clinical diagnosis for the experience of distress for people who have a marked incongruence between the gender associated with their natal sex and the gender they would like to be.

3. Modern mental health professional organizations see gender reassignment surgery as a viable way to cope with gender dysphoria.

CHAPTER 3

SCRIPTURE AND TRANSGENDERISM

Allyson Dylan Robinson is the first transgender Baptist pastor in America, and in the process has abandoned any sense of biblical authority. Born Daniel Robinson, he graduated from West Point, pastored Baptist churches in the Azores and Texas, married and had four children. While attending Truett Seminary of Baylor University from 2004 through 2007, he decided to transition to a woman. In 2014, he was reordained as a woman by Calvary Baptist Church in Washington, DC. Robinson even appeared on Bruce Jenner's show *I Am Cait* to perform a renaming ceremony for Jenner. Concerning rejection of the doctrines he learned growing up in a Southern Baptist church, Robinson said, "I have challenged nearly every doctrine that was entrusted to me and that I promised to keep on the day of my ordination. I determined to keep those only that keep me alive."[1]

Indeed, embracing a transgender identity requires a fundamental rejection of multiple biblical teachings, for Scripture teaches us to embrace our natal sex and live in a manner consistent with the basic roles associated with our sex. Scripture is more than a mere *reference point* for evaluating transgenderism: Scripture is our *starting point*, providing the true narrative and proper perspective to understand both gender and the confused feelings a person may have regarding gender.[2] A survey of Scripture's teaching about the image of God in man, the body and soul, the gift of gender, and appropriate gender behavior demonstrates how actively embracing a transgender identity (which is different from experiencing transgender temptation) is inconsistent with Christian discipleship.

HUMANS ARE MADE IN GOD'S IMAGE

The secular worldview says humans are the result of a mindless, evolutionary process and, as such, there is no inherent purpose for each person. In contrast, the Bible teaches that all people are created in the image of God and that he desires a relationship with them.[3] The structure of Genesis 1 accentuates that humans are not an afterthought or an accident emerging from random time and chance, but instead they are the pinnacle of God's creation and are given the responsibility to rule and care for the rest of God's world. Unlike plants and animals, humans are not made "after their kind." Humans are made in the image of God.[4] As such, humans are in a unique category. They are different from everything else in creation.

What does it mean to say humans are "made in God's image"? To begin, it is easier to understand what it means to be made in the image of God by eliminating some wrong ideas. First, being made in the image of God does not mean that God is like humans just a lot bigger. This sort of wrongheaded thinking is seen in popular descriptions of God as the "man upstairs." Neither does the image of God mean that humans are divine and can become a "god" someday. The first mistake leads to a retrograde view of God that diminishes his sovereignty and holiness, while the second leads to an idolatrous overestimation of humanity's potential.

With some wrong ideas cleared away, we can see that the image of God entails some definite characteristics within the makeup of humans that distinguish us from the rest of creation. These distinguishing characteristics are connected to God himself. God is love, expresses mercy, and is infinitely wise, and humans also have the capacity to express these traits. At the same time, there are certain characteristics that God retains for himself: omnipresence, omnipotence, and omniscience. As finite and created beings, we will never have God's complete attributes, but we reflect God's image when we exercise knowledge and responsible use of power for the good of his creation.[5] To be made in the image of God also means that humans reflect God's spiritual nature, for Genesis 2:7 also tells us God breathed into man the "breath of life." As a consequence of the image of God, humans have spiritual life, ethical and moral sensitivities, conscience, and the capacity to represent God.[6]

Humans: Body and Soul

As creatures made in the image of God, each human has a body and a soul. Jesus himself referenced these two aspects of human nature when he said, "Do not fear those who kill the body but are unable to kill the soul; but rather fear Him who is able to destroy both soul and body in hell" (Matt 10:28). This reality is seen in Genesis 2:7, where God personally and intimately "breathed into [Adam's] nostrils the breath of life; and man became a living being." Theologian Wayne Grudem, commenting on Genesis 2:7, says, "Here Adam is a unified person with body and soul living and acting together."[7] Christian anthropology insists we are not just a body, we are a body-soul unity, the body and soul being connected at all points.[8]

Humans: Male and Female

The gift of gender is also an intricate part of the image of God. Genesis 1:27 (ESV) says,

> God created man in his own image,
>> in the image of God he created him;
>> male and female he created them.

The Hebrew word for "man" in Genesis 1:27 is *adam*, and though it can be used as a name, here it refers to all humans. By emphasizing that God made a male *adam* and a female *adam*, Genesis 1:27 affirms that sexuality is not an accident of nature, nor is it simply a biological phenomenon. Instead, sexual identity and function are part of God's will for his image-bearers.[9] The gift of gender is not an accident of evolution or a mere social construction; it is a part of an intentional and purposeful plan for each person. When God finished the work of creation and called it "very good" (Gen 1:31), this means our gender is a very good thing to be embraced. Thus the sex we are given at birth is part of God's will for us as his image-bearers.

The purpose and plan for the two genders is made clear in Genesis 2, where the institution of marriage and the roles within marriage are made more explicit. Genesis 2 tells us God made man first, then made a "helper comparable to him" (v. 18 NKJV). While some authors wrongly see "helper" as a term of condescension, the same word is actually used several places elsewhere in the Old Testament to describe God as man's "helper" (see Pss 30:10; 54:4). As such, the term dignifies women and the female role in marriage. Of course, nonbelievers may scoff when Genesis 2:21 says God made the woman from one of man's ribs, but the truth of the narrative is really quite profound. By making Eve from Adam, God is teaching Adam to recognize a kind of mirror image of himself in Eve and thus to honor her, while Eve would see that she was made from her husband and respect his leadership.[10] In this way, gender is presented not as something arbitrary and self-defined but as an innate characteristic with corresponding role-responsibilities for each sex.

Humans: Fallen and Sinful

While every human of every race and both genders is made in God's image, the image of God has been marred by a historic fall, recorded in Genesis 3. It is the greatest of all tragedies: A real garden, a real Adam, a real Eve, a real Satan, and the very real moral and physical ruin for all of humanity. In Romans 5:12 Paul describes the devastation caused by sin: "Therefore, just as through one man sin entered into the world, and death through sin, and so death spread to all men, because all sinned." Because of the fall, our desires and wants have become distorted and idolatrous (Rom 1:18–23), and these distorted desires lead to sexual immorality and moral chaos (Rom 1:24–27).

DISORDERS OF SEXUAL DEVELOPMENT

The fall has touched creation itself, and every human body has been negatively affected. Beyond the common experience of death and decay, this means that in rare cases some people are born with bodies in which their genitalia are ambiguous, a circumstance known as a disorder of sexual development (DSD, a.k.a. intersex). Children with DSDs are also made in the image of God, and the circumstances of their birth do not mean they are worse sinners than the rest of us, nor does it mean they are somehow "cursed" by God, nor does it mean they are unloved by God. But a DSD does mean some children have unique challenges related to gender not experienced by the vast majority of us. All of us are born with fallen and flawed bodies; kids with DSDs merely deal with effects of the fall in profoundly different ways. But they too are made in the image of God and part of the world of people God loves (John 3:16).

As we saw in the previous chapter, transgender advocates try to use the existence of DSDs as proof that there is no strict gender binary, gender is fluid, and transgenderism is normal and praiseworthy. But the strength of this argument only works to the degree that DSDs and transgenderism are analogous. I suggest two significant problems with the DSD-transgender analogy. First, DSDs can be objectively diagnosed, and the causes of most such occurrences are known, often traceable to clearly known genetic problems. In contrast, no one knows what causes transgenderism, and it cannot be diagnosed in the way DSDs are. Second, a DSD is an objective diagnosis based on clearly defined and observable criteria, while transgenderism is based on a person's subjective testimony of their psychological experience. Thus I contend that there are relevant dissimilarities between DSDs and transgenderism so that the cases should be treated differently. Christians insist the God-designed gender binary is the norm, but we acknowledge rare cases of DSDs in which things don't proceed normally and view these with compassion.

GENDER-APPROPRIATE DISTINCTIONS SHOULD BE MAINTAINED

Since human nature and the environment in which we live are both inclined toward sin, there are times when people have attempted to invert gender roles, something Scripture clearly defines as sinful. The importance of maintaining healthy gender distinctions is plainly seen in Deuteronomy 22:5: "A woman shall not wear man's clothing, nor shall a man put on a woman's clothing; for whoever does these things is an abomination to the LORD your God." Though the NASB uses the same English word ("clothing") to describe the prohibition of cross-dressing for both men and women, there are actually two different Hebrew words used in the first and second clauses of the verse. The Hebrew word translated "clothing" in the first clause—"A woman shall not wear man's clothing"—is *kelî*, and it extends beyond just clothing to include vessels, receptacles, utensils, tools and implements, furniture and furnishings, and jewelry. Thus, when Deuteronomy 22:5 says women should not dress like men, it probably includes any decoration normally associated with men.[11] The Hebrew term translated "clothing" in the second half of the verse—"nor shall a man put on a woman's *clothing*"—is *simlah*, referring specifically to the outer wrapper or mantle. The point is that neither sex should make intentional attempts to deceive others concerning their natal sex. Deuteronomy 22:5 affirms that men and women should participate in gender-appropriate behavior and abstain from behavior that intends to deceive others concerning one's gender.

Deuteronomy 22:5 says cross-dressing is "an abomination to the LORD your God." The Hebrew word for "abomination" is *toevah*, a term often used to describe sexual immorality, such as in the explicit condemnation of homosexual behavior in Leviticus 18:22 and 20:13. It seems likely that homosexual behavior was associated with cross-dressing, perhaps in some cases being associated in some way with a pagan cult or ritual.[12]

Some ask, "Why is cross-dressing such a big deal? All we are discussing is clothes." While many people think the biblical prohibition of cross-dressing is obscurantist, the clothing of the cross-dresser acts as a proxy for embodiment and a corresponding rejection of God's will. The body's appearance is transformed by the clothing, cosmetics, or other accessories and paraphernalia.[13] God desires for men and women to carry themselves in such a way so that each particular gender is celebrated and easily identifiable, while taking into account certain cultural differences for gender-appropriate apparel.

Some have suggested Deuteronomy 22:5 is vague and its meaning uncertain,[14] but such claims overlook the fact that the verse is part of the Torah and assumes the worldview of Genesis 1 and 2, especially with regard to gender being part of God's good creation. Walter Kaiser, commenting on Deuteronomy 22:5 and the danger of rejecting God's parameters, says, "The tendency to obliterate all sexual distinctions often leads to licentiousness and promotes an unnaturalness opposed to God's created order."[15]

Beyond cross-dressing, the Bible also presents mutilation of the genitals in a negative light. Deuteronomy 23:1 says, "No one who is emasculated or has his male organ cut off shall enter the assembly of the LORD." While the text makes no distinction between intentional versus accidental mutilation, there are actually two categories of emasculation in Deuteronomy 23:1. The first phrase—"no one who is emasculated"—can be somewhat woodenly translated as "wounded by crushing," meaning the testicles could have been removed by crushing them or "surgically" removing them (such as surgery was in those days). The second phrase—"has his male organ cut off"—refers to a man whose penis has been cut off, a more radical step than only removing the testicles.

While many men in antiquity were castrated so they could serve as court eunuchs, there is a possibility that Deuteronomy 23:1 has pagan rites involving transgender-like behavior in view. In antiquity, in an act of pagan devotion to the goddess Ishtar, some men would cut off their penis in order to appear feminine. One ancient text criticizes "the party-boys and festival people who changed their masculinity into femininity to

make the people of Ishtar revere her. The dagger-bearer, bear-
ers of razors, pruning knives and flint blades who frequently do
abominable acts to please the heart of Ishtar."[16] Perhaps some
act like this is in the distant view of Deuteronomy 23:1. Thus
the phrase "has his male organ cut off" in Deuteronomy 23:1
may refer to a primitive attempt to present one's self as the
opposite gender.[17]

Both Deuteronomy 22:5 and 23:1 have undertones of sexual
eroticism. In the ancient Near East, ethics were often driven
by sensual pleasure, and the goal of many ancient religions
was not to bring "glory" to a particular god but to maximize
one's personal pleasure.[18] This erotic nature of paganism is seen
in Deuteronomy 23:17's strong prohibition of ritual prostitu-
tion: "None of the daughters of Israel shall be a cult prostitute,
nor shall any of the sons of Israel be a cult prostitute." Ritual
prostitutes were common in worship to pagan gods, and such
acts justified a person's sexual hedonism. In this light, both
Deuteronomy 22:5 and 23:1 could also be seen as a critique of a
sexual ethic of hedonism: People cross-dressed and men emasculated themselves for sensual reasons. In a similar way, modern
advocates of transgenderism make sexual fulfillment central to
many of their claims.

GENDER ROLES REAFFIRMED
IN THE NEW TESTAMENT

While the New Testament does not specifically address what
we today call transgenderism, the importance of maintaining
healthy gender distinctions introduced in the Old Testament is
reaffirmed in the New Testament. Most significantly, Jesus reaf-
firms the creation narrative of Genesis 1 and 2 along with the
corresponding gender binary. In a discussion about marriage
and divorce, Jesus affirmed the gender binary, saying, "But from

the beginning of creation, 'God made them male and female'" (Mark 10:6). Elsewhere in the New Testament, teachings about the roles of husbands and wives in marriage assume that people embrace the gender-appropriate role corresponding with their natal sex (Eph 5:21–33; Col 3:18–21; 1 Pet 3:1–7).[19] The concept of someone assuming a gender role different from his or her natal sex is foreign to the New Testament.

Matthew 19:12, where Jesus references three categories of eunuchs, is sometimes cited in modern discussions about transgenderism. Matthew 19:12 (ESV) says, "For there are eunuchs who have been so from birth, and there are eunuchs who have been made eunuchs by men, and there are eunuchs who have made themselves eunuchs for the sake of the kingdom of heaven. Let the one who is able to receive this receive it." The most common interpretation of these three categories among Christians with a high regard for Scripture has been that the eunuchs "from birth" refer to people who, for whatever reason, were unable to have sexual intercourse and thus did not marry; eunuchs "made by men" seems to refer to men who were intentionally emasculated, usually for the purposes of court service, as was somewhat common in antiquity; eunuchs "for the kingdom of heaven" refers to people who chose to remain unmarried for purposes of service to God.

Different authors have claimed that Matthew 19:12 addresses both DSDs and what today might be called transgenderism. Some have suggested the first category of those "born eunuchs" is a reference to people born with a DSD in which they have ambiguous genitalia. While this is certainly a possibility and I don't think it is an abuse of the text to make this suggestion, it is difficult to narrow Jesus' first category of eunuchs to this specific class of people *alone*, as the category could also possibly include congenital impotency.[20]

Some transgender activists have suggested the second category of eunuchs—"eunuchs made by men"—means in antiquity some eunuchs were considered a "third sex," somewhat like modern transgenderism.[21] This assertion is difficult to sustain on two grounds. First, ancient eunuchs were usually made so by no choice of their own, often for the purpose of serving in a harem. In contrast, in modern transgenderism people surgically alter their genitalia based on subjective psychological experience. Second, in antiquity eunuchs were still considered male, and not a "third sex": there was no innate gender dysphoria associated with being a eunuch. What is clear is that the promise of the gospel extended to eunuchs (Acts 8), and we thus certainly have good news to proclaim to modern people who have undergone gender reassignment in which they have been surgically castrated or otherwise altered.

HOMOSEXUAL BEHAVIOR FORBIDDEN IN SCRIPTURE

Many transgender people want to play the part of the opposite sex in sexual intercourse. This is homosexual behavior, which is clearly condemned in Scripture. To understand the New Testament's view of homosexuality, it is important to understand how male homosexuality was viewed in the Roman Empire of the first century. Romans believed a man should always remain dominant, both socially and sexually. While it may sound odd to modern ears, for Romans, as long as a man remained the inserting, dominant partner in a homosexual encounter and was not the one being penetrated, his masculinity was not in question. Roman assumptions about male homosexuality characterize the passive partner as somehow weak and feminine.[22] Men who took the passive or female role in homosexual sex were despised and risked losing their citizenship.[23]

This background regarding the Roman view of male homosexuality helps bring into focus Paul's reference to two specific homosexual sins in 1 Corinthians 6:9, where in a vice list of ten sins, he includes two specific words relating to homosexuality: "effeminate" and "homosexuals." The word translated "effeminate" is *malakoi*, and here it refers to the passive partner in male homosexual intercourse.[24] The word translated "homosexual" is *arsenokoitai*, and here it refers to the inserting partner in male homosexual intercourse.[25] Furthermore, the word *arsenokoitai* is clearly a term derived from the Greek translation of Leviticus 18:22 and 20:13, two explicit denunciations of homosexual behavior. In other words, Paul is saying, "I know the culture says that if a man is the dominant partner in same-sex intercourse then he's still all right. But from God's perspective, it doesn't matter which role you play, homosexual behavior is sin."[26] Included in this rule is mimicking the role of the opposite sex in intercourse.

CONTEMPORARY TRANSGENDERISM IN LIGHT OF SCRIPTURE

Modern transgenderism insists that a subjective, persistent desire to be the opposite sex should be accommodated by various means in order to achieve internal harmony, but this conclusion is inconsistent with Scripture.

As we have seen, humans are made in the image of God. While this has several implications, the most obvious is this: Because God existed before us and because we are made in God's image, a proper understanding of ourselves begins with correctly understanding God. Transgenderism as a movement inverts this order and attempts to grasp at an understanding of gender beginning with our subjective feelings. But correctly understanding gender does not begin with *us*, it begins with *God who made us*. Puritan pastor Richard Baxter (1615–1691) said: "We know little of the creature, till we know it as it stands related to the Creator."[27] Indeed, we will have a flawed understanding of gender until we understand the topic from the Creator's perspective.

Transgenderism also has a confused idea of the relationship of the soul to the body. The common claim of transgender people that "I have a male soul trapped in a female body" or a "female soul trapped in a male body" is at odds with what the Bible teaches about being made in the image of God. The soul and body are both part of God's good creation, and they are designed to complement each other. When people claim to have the soul of one gender trapped in the body of another gender, they are making a false claim based on an inadequate understanding of Christian anthropology. For people experiencing gender dysphoria, it is more accurate to say, "I am a male made in the image of God with both a body and soul, but I am experiencing confused feelings about gender right now."

Transgenderism also neglects serious discussion of the ramifications of sin and the fall. The reason people have confused feelings about gender is that we live in a fallen world corrupted by sin. All humans inherit a nature and an environment inclined toward sin.[28] Human nature is not basically good nor is it neutral: Scripture teaches our nature is to rebel against God and apart from Christ we are "dead in [our] trespasses and sins" (Eph 2:1). Because of sin, human desires are distorted and moral reflection is short-circuited. Sometimes, our broken desires include ideas about gender inconsistent with God's design. Robert Gagnon correctly says, "Human passions are notoriously unreliable indicators of God's will. 'I feel this, therefore I should be allowed to do it' would not pass muster on any viable reading of biblical ethics."[29]

Sin has also caused some people to be raised in very broken environments. Conflicted ideas about gender can emerge from painful and disturbing experiences in childhood that leave people confused about what it means to be a boy or a girl. Sexual abuse of any child is a vile sin that can reverberate decades later in a person's life as he or she tries to process the trauma of being violated, often by someone they trusted. Early and disturbing messages about sex intertwined with abuse can contribute to later confusion about gender. While not all nor even most of the people who self-identify as transgender have such tragedy in their background, such things are at least a contributing factor in the gender dysphoria some people feel.

A Christian stance acknowledges biological factors, the home environment, past experiences, and human volition can all contribute to gender dysphoria. In contrast, many modern people assert a slavish and depressing form of biological determinism as the root of transgenderism. For example, influential researchers Dick Swaab and Alicia Garcia-Falqueras say, "There is no indication that social environment after birth has an effect on gender identity or sexual orientation."[30] But in fact, these authors offer a truncated and oversimplified summary of the highly complex forces that can lead to gender dysphoria. The Christian stance is far more robust in that it acknowledges the complex matrix of variables of living in a fallen world that lead to gender confusion.

Transgenderism upends the biblical view of gender-appropriate roles connected with our natal sex. By God's design, females and males have different reproductive roles. God has designed women to give birth to children, and he has given women the ability to nurse. By design, men can accomplish neither of these tasks. Likewise, it is impossible for women to "father" children. Without the "gender binary," the world of humans does not exist. Furthermore, children should be raised in homes where a healthy distinction between the sexes is maintained, where the husband loves his wife like Christ loves the church (Eph 5:25) and where the wife respects and loves the husband (Eph 5:22–24). Taken as a whole, Scripture contradicts the idea that gender is malleable and merely a social construction.

The Roman Empire at the time of the early church was characterized by sexual promiscuity, homosexuality was common, and transgender-like behavior was acknowledged publicly. In this moral environment, Paul strongly warned the Corinthians of the dangers of sexual immorality and urged sexual restraint instead of hedonism. First Corinthians 6:18 (NKJV) says, "Flee sexual immorality. Every sin that a man does is outside the body, but he who commits sexual immorality sins against his own body." The word "flee" in 1 Corinthians 6:18 is in the present tense, suggesting that constant vigilance against sexual immorality is an ethical imperative.[31] Christians should live a lifestyle of constantly fleeing sexual immorality. In the context of 1 Corinthians, sexual purity is defined as heterosexual and monogamous marriage (7:1–7). The New Testament offers no option for transgender behavior as a legitimate form of sexual expression.

Transgenderism is also inconsistent with a Christian doctrine of the body. After telling the Corinthians to flee sexual immorality, Paul grounds his reasoning in a robust doctrine of the body and says in 1 Corinthians 6:19–20, "Or do you not know that your body is a temple of the Holy Spirit who is in you, whom you have from God, and that you are not your own? For you have been bought with a price: therefore glorify God in your body." The way Christians treat the body was not left up to one's own moral autonomy but was intended to be used consistent with the creation paradigm as presented in Genesis: Paul advocates healthy appreciation of one's natal sex and appropriate sexual expression within heterosexual and monogamous marriage. God holds us morally accountable for what we do with and to our body. In this light, modern surgical mutilation of genitals for the purposes of mimicking the opposite sex should be rejected.

Transgenderism is associated with meaninglessness and a fundamental rejection of reality as ordered by God. For example, transgender activist Nicholas Teich says, "There is no getting around the fact that the gender binary of men and women—as we always knew it—is not the reality."[32] One is left to wonder how Teich believes he came into the world *apart from the gender binary*.

The biblical worldview invites people to embrace reality: God made the universe; God made humans for a purpose; sin distorts our purpose; Jesus Christ died and rose again to forgive sin and give hope to broken people. While the modern embrace of the transgender narrative can seem intimidating, the biblical narrative of creation, fall, and redemption is far more coherent and internally consistent than the confused arguments of those who see our world as something to be molded to one's subjective whims.

We began this chapter with the story of pastor Daniel Robinson's transition to Allyson Dylan Robinson. Robinson claims an inner voice told him, "What if the Bible is wrong? What if you've been reading it wrong?" Robinson's "inner voice" has a distinct echo of Satan himself in Genesis 3:1, when he questioned God's authority, asking, "Has God said?" In this light, we see that at the heart of any discussion of transgenderism is the issue of the truthfulness of God's word. Each of us is broken by sin, and regardless of our subjective feelings, God's word gives us the true perspective to make a moral evaluation of temptation.

KEY POINTS

1. Being made male and female is an intricate part of being made in the image of God.

2. The gift of gender is part of the goodness of God's creation.

3. Embracing a transgender identity is inconsistent with Christian ethics.

CHAPTER 4

GENETICS AND TRANSGENDERISM

The halftime show at Super Bowl LI on February 5, 2017, featured pop sensation Lady Gaga (Stefani Angelina Germanotta). After a dramatic dive into the stadium from the roof, she sang a medley of some of her most popular songs, including her 2011 monster hit "Born This Way," a song that has set the boundaries for moral discussion about gender and sexuality for many young people. In one of the most popular lines from the song, she croons, "No matter, gay, straight, or bi / Lesbian, transgendered life / I'm on the right track, baby I was born to survive." The song then quickly parallels these various sexual and gender identities with ethnicity, equating gender with being black or white. The catchy chorus says, "I'm on the right track, baby I was born this way!"[1] For our purposes, it is important to note the way Lady Gaga equates being transgender with being born of a particular race. For many people, transgenderism is seen in just this way: it is a trait with which some people are born and is similar to hair, eye, and skin color.

A careful review of research regarding genetics and transgenderism reveals that transgenderism is not an inherited trait like skin color. Instead, current research demonstrates that while genetic variations may serve as *contributing factors* to the complex identity known as transgenderism, the evidence that transgenderism is *caused* by genetics is quite weak. This distinction between a contributing factor and causation is essential: A contributing factor increases the likelihood that something may happen; causation means that something produces a definite effect. As we will see, to date, no studies have found specific genes that cause transgenderism. To demonstrate this, I will summarize the prenatal hormone theory regarding transgenderism, briefly discuss the genetic complexity of most traits, review genetic research related to transgenderism, and briefly explore epigenetics and transgenderism.

THE PRENATAL HORMONE THEORY OF TRANSGENDERISM

No one knows what causes gender dysphoria and transgenderism, but the most common suggestion is the prenatal hormone theory, which says transgenderism arises in the womb from a discrepancy between sexual differentiation of the genitals and sexual differentiation of the brain. In the womb, the genitals develop first and the brain experiences sexual differentiation later. Thus, this theory suggests that, early on in prenatal development, the genitalia of someone who is "transgender" develops in accordance with his or her genetic sex, but then an aberration occurs and later the brain develops in a manner consistent with the opposite sex, resulting in someone who claims to have a "male" body with a "female" brain or a "female" body with a "male" brain. This theory is central to both genetic and brain research regarding the origins of transgenderism.[2]

MOST TRAITS ARE THE RESULT OF MORE THAN ONE GENE

Before I summarize genetic research on transgenderism, it is important to remember that most traits are the result of more than one gene. For example, scientists used to think eye color was determined by a single gene. Brown eyes, for example, were always considered dominant to blue. It is now known that the inheritance patterns for eye color are much more complex and involve several genes.[3] Because a relatively simple trait like eye color is the result of several genes interacting, if a behavioral trait like transgenderism is genetic, it will likely be even more complex, which also means it will be difficult for researchers to pinpoint and accurately identify the specific genetic variables involved.

TRANSGENDERISM AND GENES RELATED TO ANDROGEN AND ESTROGEN RECEPTORS

If the prenatal hormone theory is true, some argue that the reason the brain develops inconsistently with the genitals is related to the genes for androgen receptors and estrogen receptors. Among the many aspects of the amazing human body God has designed, androgen and estrogen receptors are special proteins that have a tremendous influence over our sex. In general, receptor proteins serve as the "eyes and ears" of cells, receiving messages from substances in the bloodstream and then telling the cells what to do.[4] In boys, androgen receptors are an essential component of male sexual differentiation in the womb and later changes during puberty.[5] Likewise, in girls, estrogen receptors are an essential component of female sexual differentiation in the womb and during puberty. Because androgen and estrogen receptors are so important in sexual development, some researchers have tried to discover if transgender people have unique genes related to this process that might *cause* them to be transgender. Because testosterone (an androgen) and estrogen are essential to the normal development of males and females, it makes sense to examine genes that affect the way the body processes these hormones if one thinks transgenderism has a genetic cause.

A 2005 study of 29 transsexuals in Sweden claimed to find a weak link between changes in estrogen receptor genes and MtF transsexualism. Specifically, the researchers were hoping to find small changes in DNA base pairs called "polymorphisms," which may influence gender development. The researchers claimed that certain repeated sequences of DNA in the estrogen receptor genes of MtF transsexuals differed from non-transsexuals. But they qualified their finding by saying that the results should be "interpreted with utmost caution."[6] They also admitted that the genes they examined were not the primary cause of transgenderism, saying, "Whereas transsexualism is a very rare condition, the gene variants investigated in this study are relatively common; none of the studied variants could hence be assumed to be a primary cause of [transsexualism]."[7]

Other efforts to prove that genes related to hormone receptors cause transgenderism have yielded contradictory findings. A 2009 Australian study of 112 MtF transsexuals claimed to find an association between changes in the androgen receptor gene and MtF transsexuals, but could not replicate the findings from the 2005 study regarding the estrogen receptor gene and transsexualism.[8] In 2009, Japanese researchers studied 74 MtF transsexuals and 168 FtM transsexuals and could find no significant differences in either androgen receptor or estrogen receptor genes between transsexuals and controls. The authors say, "The present findings do not provide any evidence that genetic variants of sex hormone-related genes confer individual susceptibility to MtF or FtM transsexualism."[9] In 2014, genetic researchers from Spain could find no evidence of an association between sex-hormone-related genes and MtF transsexualism, but the same group did claim to find an association between an estrogen receptor gene and FtM transsexualism.[10] The sample for this last study was large and well organized, but there was overlap in the data between the transsexuals and the control group, meaning they discovered *correlation* but not causation.

Research on genes related to androgen receptors and estrogen receptors in MtF and FtM transsexuals had yielded widely divergent results, though some findings are intriguing. The results are contradictory; nothing has been proved conclusively concerning these particular genes and transgender identity.

CYP17 GENE

A flurry of genetic research regarding transgenderism has been focused on the CYP17A1 gene, which provides instructions for making enzymes important in the formation of sex hormones. In 2009, a study of German and Austrian transsexuals claimed certain changes in CYP17A1 gene were associated with FtM transsexualism, but not MtF cases. Specifically, they claimed that some of the FtM transsexuals—who are born biologically female—had specific genetic patterns that looked more like people born biologically male.[11] A 2015 study from Spain of the same gene claimed to find similar results and said their data "might suggest" some hypothetical involvement of the CYP17A1 gene in transsexualism,[12] but one year later the same group published another study on the same gene could find no connection to transgenderism and said the new data "contradict previous findings" about this region of DNA.[13] Nothing conclusive has been proved about the CYP17 gene and transgenderism.

SRD5A2 GENE AND TRANSGENDERISM

Another candidate gene for causing transgenderism is known as SRD5A2, a gene that provides instructions for making an enzyme involved in processing androgens, which are hormones that direct male sexual development.[14] Because of the gene's connection to male sexual differentiation, in 2007 a group of researchers from the Netherlands and Austria hypothesized that particular changes in this gene would be common in MtF trans sexuals and underrepresented in FtM transsexuals. The team examined the DNA of 104 MtF transsexuals, 49 FtM transsexuals, 755 non-transgender men, and 915 non-transgender women. The researchers found no significant difference in the SRD5A2 gene of any of the transsexuals when compared with controls. They concluded by saying the SRD5A2 gene "is not significantly associated with FtM and MtF transsexualism."[15] In other words, variations in this gene are not the cause of transgenderism.

FAMILY STUDIES, TWIN STUDIES, AND TRANSGENDERISM

Some studies have claimed that family members of transgender people are more likely to be transgender themselves, thus demonstrating a genetic component at work in transgenderism. But actually, cases where multiple family members are transgender are rare. For example, a 2010 study of 995 transsexuals (677 MtF; 318 FtM) found only twelve cases of siblings who were also transsexual. Though this study indicated that a higher percentage of siblings of transsexuals are also transsexual when compared to the general population, the chance of two siblings being so is quite low.[16] The overwhelming majority of those with transgender siblings are not transgender. In fact, the great majority of transgender adults are unaware of other transgender people in their families, pointing to the limited explanatory power of genetic arguments for transgenderism.[17] Also, the shared family environments make it difficult to disentangle genetic and environmental explanations for siblings who are transgender.[18]

Findings related to twin studies and transgenderism indicate that genetics may play a contributing role, but are far from determinative. A 2011 British study of 4,426 female twins discovered a very low influence of genes for gender identity and gender dysphoria.[19] A 2012 review of a small sample of twin pairs found that of 23 identical twin pairs (including female twin pairs and male twin pairs), there were nine cases (39.1 percent) where both twins experienced gender identity disorder (GID); in contrast, none of the 21 pairs of same-sex nonidentical twins shared GID, a statistically significant difference.[20]

How do we interpret the twin data? First and foremost, if transgenderism were a trait like hair and skin color, then in every case where one sibling is transgender, his or her identical twin would be as well. But second, the fact that none of the nonidentical twins shared GID but several of the identical twins did indicates some genetic variable may possibly contribute to transgenderism. Overall, family and twin studies to date indicate a weak to slightly modest genetic component to transgenderism in some specific cases.

To summarize, the evidence is weak concerning possible candidate genes for transgenderism. Dutch researchers Daniel Klink and Martin Den Heijer of Leiden University are both supportive of transgenderism, yet even they say, "Hitherto, no strong candidate gene has emerged for the development of gender dysphoria. Because of the complexity of gender identity development, it does not seem likely that one single gene will be discovered."[21] Future research will likely focus on possible ways multiple genes interact to influence transgenderism.

EPIGENETICS AND TRANSGENDERISM

Epigenetics, a burgeoning field of scientific research, is now a growing focus of research into possible avenues of biological determination regarding transgenderism. "Epigenetics" refers to chemical modifications of the human genome that alter gene activity without changing the DNA sequence. DNA is wrapped around proteins called histones, and both DNA and the histones are covered with chemical "tags." These histones and chemical tags (or "epi-marks") are part of each person's epigenetics, constituting an extra layer of information attached to our genes' backbones that regulates their expression.[22] As science has discovered more and more about genetic traits, we have learned that these epigenetic structures regulate genome activity and govern which genes in the DNA of any given cell will be active. These epigenetic structures can be thought of as switches and knobs that turns things "on or off" or "up and down." Perhaps the most fascinating difference between DNA and epigenetics is that the genome does not change during cell division throughout a person's lifetime; but the epigenome can change, and these changes can be influenced by our lifestyles.

Author Nessa Carey suggests that a helpful analogy for understanding epigenetics is to think of actors reading a script for a movie.[23] For example, Director Baz Luhrmann hands Leonardo DiCaprio his shortened version of Shakespeare's script for *Romeo and Juliet*, on which Luhrmann has written or typed various notes—such as directions for camera placements and other technical information. Whenever DiCaprio's copy of the script is photocopied, Luhrmann's additional information is copied along with it. Claire Danes, playing the part of Juliet, also has a script for *Romeo and Juliet*. While the notes on her copy are different from those on DiCaprio's, Danes's notes will also survive photocopying. Carey explains, "That's how epigenetic regulation of gene expression occurs—different cells have the same DNA blueprint (the original author's script) but carrying varied molecular modifications (the shooting script) which can be transmitted from mother cell to daughter cell during cell division."[24]

Do epigenetics explain transgenderism? Hard proof for such a theory is lacking, the main evidence being a 2000 report which claimed that MtF transsexuals have a significant excess of maternal aunts versus uncles. The authors suggest that the epigenetic mechanisms may be at work in this anomaly.[25] Yet, this study found no abnormal number of paternal aunts or uncles for FtM transsexuals, thus based on their own data the claimed epigenetic mechanism only offers insight into one form of transgenderism and is not a global explanation. More problematically, the study has not been replicated since its publication in 2000.

In spite of the paucity of evidence, transgender author Thomas E. Bevan, a former psychology professor at Georgia Tech, commented in 2015, "There is positive evidence that epigenetics are a causal factor in transsexualism and transgenderism, but at this point it is only suggestive that future research should be conducted."[26] But the evidence Bevan presents at best points to epigenetics as a possible *contributing factor*, not a *causative* factor. Klink and Den Heijer admit the biological evidence for an epigenetic causation for transgenderism is lacking, but then exclaim that "it does offer a new perspective to investigate sex chromosome effects in brain differentiation."[27] In other words, no epigenetic cause for transgenderism has yet been found, but some researchers hope one will be discovered.

In fact, future research may indicate that the epigenome is actually *changed by transgenderism*. Scientists are still exploring and discovering the degree to which the epigenome itself can be changed by human choices. Research into alcoholism and epigenetics gives some perspective on what could possibly be discovered regarding transgenderism. A robust body of evidence strongly indicates that alcoholism can lead to epigenetic changes that actually strengthen the alcoholism itself. An emerging model suggests that some genetic factors may predispose some people to alcoholism. These genetic factors are accentuated because epigenetic changes can be induced by alcohol, which modifies gene expression. These changes encourage further alcohol use and ultimately contribute to addiction.[28] I suggest we should be open to the possibility that something similar may occur in transgenderism. People who engage in transgender behavior may find that the behavior itself is reinforced by epigenetic changes brought on by the behavior itself.[29] In this way, transgenderism may become compulsive and feel quite "natural." But at present, such theories are speculative since conclusive evidence for an epigenetic contribution to transgenderism has not been discovered.

CONCLUSION: GENETICS AND TRANSGENDERISM

No one has yet discovered a "transgender" gene, nor have any genetic or epigenetic factors been discovered that are both necessary and sufficient to cause transgenderism. Laura-Erickson Schroth of New York University summarizes genetics research and transgenderism, saying, "To date, no studies have conclusively linked genes to transgender identity."[30] She also comments that the findings of the various studies are statistically significant, but the differences in the various findings have been difficult to replicate. She added, "Together, genetic studies provide some support that genetic variations in hormones could play a role in shaping gender identity in some people."[31]

Since multiple genes are involved in most human traits, it would be surprising to find *one* gene that causes transgenderism. Some combination of genes may be involved as a contributing factor in transgenderism for some people, but this is far different from saying transgender people are "born this way," nor does it mean that people are predetermined to be transgender. Instead, genetics serves as one component of a complex matrix of factors leading to transgenderism. As costs of full DNA scans continue to decrease, one can expect much more research in this area in coming decades.

Scientific evidence to date clearly does not show the existence of a gene or genes that *cause* transgenderism. Instead, changes to a few limited regions within the human genome demonstrate a low level of correlation with a transgender identity. The simplistic "born this way" argument regarding transgenderism is inconsistent with current scientific research. The Christian view is more robust and suggests that transgenderism emerges from a complex matrix of factors including one's genetics, family of origin, environment, response to stress and temptation, and perhaps many other factors that remain unknown to us.

I admit there is possibly a genetic component to transgenderism, much as there is a genetic component to every human behavior. But this is not the same as saying our actions are genetically predetermined: Human behavior, especially complex behavior like transgenderism, is not *genetically hardwired* and is not a trait like hair or skin color. At the same time, if some hypothetical future study did indeed find a gene or combination of genes that guaranteed someone would experience gender dysphoria, this would not excuse such people from moral accountability any more than people experiencing other temptations with a genetic component—alcoholism, drug abuse—are excused from moral accountability. As a consequence of the fall in Genesis 3, all of creation has been negatively affected, even our genetics. In this light, Christians should not be surprised that genetics are a contributing factor in many temptations, including transgenderism.

Even within investigations into transgenderism and genetics, we should not overlook the worldview assumptions underlying some of the assertions. For example, Bevan insists that transgenderism is a biologically determined trait, but in the middle of his discussion he makes a worldview claim: "The continuous visible world we see is an illusion," and he adds that "conscious choice is also an illusion."[32] If Bevan's claim that the world we see is an illusion is true, one is left to wonder why he thinks anyone should take what he says seriously or why he thinks two people could have a coherent discussion about transgenderism or anything else.

Research to date *has not found a transgender gene*. Theories in any field that are the most helpful and robust are ones that help *predict* future incidences of a trait occurring. In any field, experiments are performed to help make predictions and verify them based on accumulated data. To date, genetic research concerning transgenderism has virtually no predictive power: It is impossible to perform a DNA test on a child in utero and determine if he or she will be transgender. But in some limited populations and sample groups, there may be some genetic variables that when combined with other factors and the consequences of human choice may contribute to a higher incidence of transgenderism in limited circumstance. Again, this is a completely different assertion from saying, "I'm born this way."

Every choice we make living on planet Earth has a genetic component at some level. From a scriptural viewpoint, humans are fabulously complex creatures who exercise and direct their desires toward chosen goals. At the same time, the vicissitudes of life may lead some people to experience the temptation of transgenderism, to adopt the identity of the opposite gender, and to embrace a transgender identity. Quite often, this is a temptation for which the person did not ask. But regardless of the source of temptation, we are not excused from moral account-ability. In Genesis 3, Adam blamed Eve for his failure and even subtly blamed God, referring to Eve as "the woman you [God] gave me." Eve then blamed the serpent. This pattern has been repeated throughout human history: we shift blame to other factors when we succumb to temptation and sin. While genetics and epigenetics are contributing factors in the moral lives of every human, we are not excused from moral accountability because of these variables.

KEY POINTS

1. Some research indicates a weak correlation between a few genetic differences and transgenderism. Correlation does not equal causation.

2. No one has found a transgender gene.

3. Because of the fall, Christians should not be surprised if genetics is a contributing factor to temptation.

CHAPTER 5

THE BRAIN AND TRANSGENDERISM

One of the most well-known transgender people in America is Chaz Bono, born as the daughter named Chastity Bono to famous singing duo Sonny Bono and Cher. Attempting to explain transgenderism, Bono said, "I think of it as hormones that, you know, went in the brain but not in the body, and that's all being transgender is. It's just that the sex of your body and the gender of the brain don't match up."[1] Bono is articulating a form of the prenatal hormone theory (introduced in the last chapter), which suggests that, early on in prenatal development, the genitalia of someone who is transgender develops in accordance with his or her genetic sex, but then an aberration occurs and later the brain develops in a manner consistent with the opposite sex. The theory claims transgenderism is rooted in brain differences caused by atypical prenatal hormone exposure.

Do transgender people have brains that are fundamentally different from their biological sex? In what follows, we will see that though there have

been some interesting discoveries, no distinctive brain difference between transgender people and non-transgender people
has been conclusively demonstrated. Current data show a correlation between some variables in the brains of some people
and an increased rate of transgenderism. But correlation and
causation are not the same thing, and *causation* has not been
proved. To explain these ideas, I will begin with a brief survey
of the brain and gender, and then discuss various claims regarding transgenderism and brain differences.

GENDER DIFFERENCES IN THE HUMAN BRAIN

To what degree are male and female brains actually different?
While finding consensus about the exact gender differences in
our brains can be daunting, we must emphasize that the brains
of men and women are far more alike than they are different.
Men and women have the same structures located in the same
places within the brain, and the same capacity for intelligence.
To say there are gender differences in the brain does not mean
women have a brain component men don't have, or vice versa.[2]

Competing and contradictory assertions about gender differences in the brain abound, but several claims are commonly
accepted within the scientific community.[3] The most consistently proved difference between male and female brains is
that males have a larger brain volume, with male volume rang-
ing 8 to 13 percent larger than females.[4] Another difference
is that, as a general rule, women have a higher percentage of
"gray" matter—tissue containing neurons, which are essential
for thinking—while male brains have a higher percentage of
"white" matter—tissue composed of axons, nerve fibers extend-
ing from neurons that connect the various components of the
brain like a networking grid.[5] The amygdala size also seems
to show some difference and is usually larger in males than

females.[6] Furthermore, others suggest a sex difference exists in amygdala activity such that in men the activity in the right amygdala predicts subsequent memory, but in women the activity in the left amygdala does.[7] Other claims about sex-related brain differences abound, but the ones mentioned here give a sufficient idea of the types that are generally accepted.[8]

These findings noted, the differences between the brains of men and women are more limited than what most people think of when trying to conceptualize a "male" brain versus a "female" brain. Furthermore, there is overlap in the data between men and women, and the claims that are made are based on averages. Many sex-specific differences have often been exaggerated by purveyors of pop psychology and the popular media.[9] Differences in particular structures that have been identified are often differences in volume, shape, or connectivity. These points of clarification are quite important to keep in mind when discussing the possibility of a transgender brain: Even if such a thing exists, the differences would likely be limited in a manner similar to the differences between males and females. But as we will see, there is even more debate and less definitive evidence regarding a purported transgender brain. I will now review arguments about suggested transgender brain differences related to intracranial volume, the INAH 3, the bed nucleus of the stria terminalis, and differences in gray versus white matter.

NO DIFFERENCE IN BRAIN VOLUME FOR TRANSGENDERS

The most easily identifiable difference between male and female brains is that men on average have a greater intracranial volume. But research to date does not show that transgender people have a brain volume different from their natal sex. Two different studies have shown no significant difference in the brain volume for transgender males when compared to other males.[10]

TRANSGENDERISM AND THE INAH 3

The interstitial nucleus of the anterior hypothalamus 3 (INAH 3) is a small cluster of cells in the hypothalamus. In 1991, Simon LeVay, a neuroscientist associated with the prestigious Salk Institute for Biological Studies, made two major claims about INAH 3: (1) The INAH 3 in heterosexual men is larger than in women, and (2) the INAH 3 of homosexual men is closer in size to women than heterosexual men. Thus, he suggested a smaller INAH 3 size led to male homosexuality.[11] In 2008, Dutch researchers Alicia Garcia-Falgueras and Dick Swaab claimed to make a similar discovery regarding the INAH 3 of transsexuals. First, they claimed that the INAH 3 in fourteen heterosexual males was about twice as large as in eleven heterosexual females. Then they claimed that the INAH 3 in eleven MtF transsexuals was similar in size to women. Garcia-Falgueras and Swaab strongly suggested the differences they noted were prenatal in origin, meaning transsexuals are "born this way."[12] Taken together, the studies claim both sexual orientation and gender identity are related to INAH 3 volume.

While LeVay's research is frequently cited in born-this-way arguments regarding homosexuality, a close reading of his data reveals that more care should be exercised before making extravagant claims based on the INAH 3. In LeVay's own sample, there was overlap in his data: Some heterosexual men had an INAH 3 closer in size to the majority of the homosexuals, and some homosexuals had an INAH 3 closer in size to the majority of the heterosexuals, meaning a particular INAH 3 size is neither necessary nor sufficient to cause homosexuality. And in fact, the data concerning the INAH 3 and transsexuals shows much the same thing: One heterosexual male had the same INAH 3 size as four of the smallest transsexuals, and some of the transsexuals had an INAH 3 size and volume similar to the majority of the heterosexual males. A particular INAH 3 size is neither necessary nor sufficient to cause transgenderism. Furthermore, in the years since both studies, there has yet to be unambiguous replication of the data.

Additionally, the transsexuals had been taking cross-sex hormones, which may have affected their INAH 3 size, a claim the researchers rejected.[13] But there are questions about how transgender hormone therapy affects the brain itself. Typically, males have a larger brain volume than females, but both sexes have the same number of neurons. A 2006 Dutch study suggested hormone therapy for transsexuals affects brain volume in both MtF and FtM. Though the sample was small, with only eight MtF and six FtM, the researchers concluded that in young adults, "androgen treatment increases the volume of the female brain towards male proportions and anti-androgen + estrogen treatment reduces the size of the male brain towards female proportions. The findings imply plasticity of adult human brain structure towards the opposite sex under the influence of cross-sex hormones."[14] Similarly, a 2014 study of fifteen FtM and fourteen MtF found that cortical thickness changed in both groups after hormonal treatment, with their brains shifting to a pattern similar to the opposite sex.[15] The use of cross-sex hormones appears to induce changes in the brain, and it is possible such changes do not reverse with the cessation of hormonal therapy. Thus, it is possible that data on the INAH 3 was also influenced by the use of cross-sex hormones.

BED NUCLEUS OF THE STRIA TERMINALIS AND TRANSGENDERISM

The bed nucleus of the stria terminalis (BNST) is a sort of complex relay center in the brain, with neurocircuits coordinating the contributions of different systems into organized physiological functions and behaviors. Some have suggested that among many sources of information, the BNST interacts with sexual hormone levels.[16] Among many functions, the BNST is also strongly connected to sustained states of fear,[17] social attachment behavior, and initiating of mating along with partner preference.[18] Some researchers have suggested the BNST may play a role in transgenderism.

Dutch physician and scientist Dick Swaab is one of the most influential researchers in the world regarding homosexuality, transgenderism, and brain research. In 1995, his team claimed that a particular part of the BNST called the central subdivision is larger in men than in women and that in MtF transsexuals it is female-sized.[19] Swaab's team concludes by saying, "Our study supports the hypothesis that gender identity alterations may develop as a result of an altered interaction between the development of the brain and sex hormones."[20]

Swaab's claims concerning the BNST have several limitations. First, his sample consisted of forty-two cadavers, only six of whom were transsexuals. It is quite incautious to make global claims based on a sample of *six* transsexuals. Furthermore, two heterosexual males in his sample had a central subdivision of the BNST size that fell into the range of size for transsexuals, meaning a certain size of this brain structure is not sufficient to cause transsexualism.[21] Another confounding factor in the research is that all six of the transsexuals in this study had taken female hormones as adults as part of their process of transitioning from male to female. Swaab and colleagues acknowledged the possibility that the reduced size of the BNST "could possibly have been due to the presence of high levels of [estrogen] in the blood," but they discount this possibility because two of the transsexuals had stopped taking estrogen prior to their death.[22] But the researchers seem to overlook the possibility that taking estrogen as an adult introduces permanent changes that cannot be reversed merely by ceasing to take estrogen. In other words, the differences in the BNST may be because the transsexuals took female hormones as an adult, and not because of an innate difference in their anatomy present from birth.

In a follow-up study published in 2000, Swaab asserted that the number of neurons in the BNST in transsexuals more closely resembled women than men. But much like his previous study, Swaab's own data poses some questions regarding his claim. Two heterosexual males had a neuronal number more similar to the transsexuals, and one transsexual had a neuronal number more similar to the heterosexual males.[23] This demonstrates that in Swaab's own sample a particular neuronal number within the BNST was neither necessary nor sufficient to cause transgenderism. And again, his sample was very small, consisting only of six transsexuals.

A study published in 2002 by Swaab's team further complicated findings regarding purported differences in BNST and transgenderism. Studying fifty brains postmortem, they discovered that there does tend to be a size difference in this area of the brain between males and females, but size differentiation between men and women became significant only in adulthood: there were no statistically significant differences in size among children.[24] The authors offered different scenarios in which their new findings might still be consistent with prenatal hormonal differentiation of the brain, but also concluded by saying the changes in "volume in male-to-female transsexuals may be the result of a failure to develop a male-like gender identity." They added that the fact that these differences are only observable in adulthood "suggests that marked sex-dependent organizational changes in brain structure are not limited to early development but may extend into adulthood."[25] In other words, the phenomenon of a size difference in the BNST between heterosexual males and MtF transsexuals may be more of an effect than a cause.

GRAY MATTER, WHITE MATTER, AND TRANSGENDER AS A "THIRD" BRAIN TYPE

As was noted earlier, female brains typically have a higher percentage of gray matter than those of males. Some researchers have argued that transgender people actually constitute a third brain type and have an identifiable pattern of gray matter to white matter different from males or females. But the limited number of studies on the topic contradict each other. For example, in 2011 researchers from Spain claimed to have found specific differences in the white matter of both MtF and FtM transsexuals,[26] but in 2014 other researchers using the same methods were unable to replicate the Spanish findings.[27] As a result, the results of these two groups diverge so substantially that no reliable conclusion can be made so far.[28]

EVALUATION OF BRAIN RESEARCH AND TRANSGENDERISM

Some researchers claim transgender people have a unique brain type, with one group saying, "Untreated MtFs and FtMs who have an early onset of their gender dysphoria and are sexually oriented to persons of their natal sex show a distinctive brain morphology, reflecting a brain phenotype."[29] Milton Diamond of the University of Hawaii goes even further, saying,

"The evidence, I believe, is strong enough to consider trans-sexuality to be a form of brain intersex."[30] In other words, the transgender brain is a *third type*, different from both males and females. Claims of this magnitude should be supported by incontrovertible evidence, but a closer look gives some pause before we assume science has proved transgender people were born with a different brain which causes their gender dysphoria. Problems include limitations associated with brain imaging studies related to behavioral research, the effects of brain plasticity, the manner in which the data is interpreted, and the degree to which there is substantial overlap in much of the data.

Neuroimaging has fantastically broadened medicine's ability to diagnose brain disease and trauma, but when neuroimaging is used in research on behavioral traits, it has inherent limitations. Lawrence Mayer and Paul McHugh explain, "When the trait in question is not a concrete behavior but something as elusive and vague as 'gender identity,' these methodological problems are even more serious."[31] To achieve proof of causation, neuroimaging studies would need to follow a particular cohort of fixed individuals across the course of their sexual development if not their entire lifespan.[32] No study has even approached such comprehensive research.

Brain plasticity refers to the manner in which the human brain builds new pathways between neurons and discards old connections. This is another variable to consider when evaluating research on transgenderism and the brain. Choices we make can modify our brain. While it is a vast oversimplification to suggest all of the differences I have discussed in gray matter and white matter are the result of brain plasticity, at the same time we must not overlook the degree to which the human *will* affects our brain—choices we make matter and become self-reinforcing, a pattern that emerges in the very way our neurons are connected within the brain. Brain plasticity may affect findings regarding brain research and transgenderism.

Closely related to the issue of brain plasticity is the question of how the data should be interpreted. The gist of research on transgenderism and the brain seems to be that the researchers think they have found inborn differences that explain why people are transgender. But it is not immediately obvious if the differences are inborn or appear later. Are these differences caused by prenatal or postnatal factors? To what degree do issues of socialization and family structure interact with purported brain differences? Furthermore, it is not clear how the purported brain differences would affect one's sense of gender or sexual orientation. The research to date cannot answer these questions, though the authors all tend to emphasize the roles of hormones in organization of the brain.

Finally, a healthy analysis of the data will also acknowledge overlap in the findings: Some of the transsexuals had measurements that fell into the normal range for their sex; some of the heterosexual males and females had measurements that overlapped with some of the transsexuals. A particular pattern of gray-matter or white-matter organization is neither necessary nor sufficient to cause transgenderism. Researchers *may* have found some variables in the brain that are possibly a contributing factor to transgenderism. But this is a far cry from finding a trait that is a cause.

The degree to which various factors affect the brain can be seen in recent research suggesting that socioeconomic status affects the thickness of gray matter. One group of researchers claimed that lower socioeconomic status is associated with a steep decrease in cortical thickness in early childhood, while children from a higher socioeconomic status were not associated with such steep decreases.[33] Certainly no one thinks this data means some children are "born to be poorer than others." No, this data simply points out the manner in which external factors affect brain development. External factors likely affect the brain development in transgender people as well.

The fact is, there are numerous variations in the cortical thickness of men and women within the general population, with much overlap in the data. For example, a 2017 study of MRIs from 5,216 people in the United Kingdom found that on average women exhibited thicker cortices (gray matter) than males. But the researchers go on to say, "Overall, for every brain region that showed even large sex differences, there was always overlap between males and females, confirming that the human brain cannot—at least for the measures observed here—be described as "sexually dimorphic."[34] If the human brain cannot be considered "sexually dimorphic" in the same way genitalia are dimorphic, one is hard-pressed to accept that there is in fact such a thing as a transgender brain. A balanced approach admits limited differences between male and female brains without making exaggerated assertions.

THE CAUSE OF TRANSGENDERISM IS UNKNOWN

After reviewing data concerning the causes of transgenderism, we can conclude that the causes of transgenderism are unknown, but hormonal, genetic, brain organization, and environmental variables are all likely to be contributing factors. But this is far, far different from saying transgenderism is caused by any innate characteristic or that transgender people are "born this way." While research certainly has more to learn regarding the brains of transgender people, current data do not prove a third brain type exists.

What many are actually arguing for regarding transgenderism is a harsh form of biological determinism. For example, in 2013, Milton Diamond said, "These findings offer additional evidence to indicate that transsexualism has a biologic, nervous-system component strong enough to say that gender identity may be less a matter of choice and more a matter of biology."[35] Likewise, in 2009, Swaab and Garcia-Falgueras argued transgenderism resulted from variations in prenatal hormone exposure to the brain and said there is "no proof that the social environment after birth has an effect on the development of gender or sexual orientation."[36]

But does the data really support an extreme form of biological determinism regarding transgenderism? The studies reviewed here demonstrate a biological *component* as a contributing factor to transgenderism. But acknowledging a biological component is a far cry from affirming biological determinism. Christians do not deny biology can play a role in the life experiences of everyone. Indeed, we are sensitive to our own temperaments and inclinations, and successful growth in our walk with Jesus Christ requires us to be self-aware of the way these can make us susceptible to different temptations. What Christians do reject is biological determinism, which says humans are merely highly evolved chemical machines that have learned how to self-reflect. Beyond this, in the various studies of transgender brains, often it is not clear the degree to which participation in transgender behavior or use of cross-sex hormones has modified the brain leading to observable changes. Thus certainly Diamond and others should show more modesty before asserting the existence of a transgender brain.

At the same time, the biological and genetic components of transgenderism seem significant enough in some people that we as Christians should acknowledge they did not *choose* to experience gender dysphoria. For someone wrestling with confused ideas about gender, it can be comforting to hear, "I don't think you *asked for* gender dysphoria." Currently, though several contributing factors are emerging as important, we simply do not know why people experience gender confusion. Our friends deserve mercy as they navigate what may in many cases be unwanted or unexpected feelings. Yet Christian mercy operates within the parameters of God's purpose for creation, and we cannot in the name of mercy affirm gender transition or transgender behavior, especially when highly debated notions of a "transgender brain" are central to some of the arguments.

KEY POINTS

1. A particular INAH 3 size is neither necessary nor sufficient to cause transgenderism.

2. Research claiming that a particular BNST size causes transgenderism has not been replicated.

3. Studies regarding the percentage of gray matter to white matter in the brains of transgender people contradict each other.

4. It is difficult to know if some of the purported differences in the brains of transgender people actually cause transgenderism or are the result of transgenderism.

5. The use of cross-sex hormones may be affecting some of the data on purported differences in the brains of transgender people.

6. No one knows what causes transgenderism.

CHAPTER 6

HORMONAL TREATMENT OF GENDER DYSPHORIA

Perhaps the most well-known transgender child in America is Jazz Jennings. Born a male in 2000, Jazz was diagnosed with gender identity disorder in 2004 and has since adopted a female identity. In 2011, the Oprah Winfrey Network broadcast *I Am Jazz: A Family in Transition*, a program that relates how Jazz's family coped with gender transition. Jennings has subsequently published the book *I Am Jazz* (2013) and stars in the reality TV series by the same name (2015).

As part of Jazz's transition to a female identity, the child was given drugs to suppress the normal progression of puberty; thus Jazz never developed male secondary sex characteristics. In 2017, Jennings indicated a desire to have gender reassignment surgery (GRS). In male-to-female (MtF) GRS, the penis is often used to create an artificial vagina. But in Jazz's case, the normal growth of genitalia that happens in puberty has not occurred because he was taking puberty-suppressing drugs, leading to difficulties for potential GRS. Jennings said, "There's some problems because I've been on the hormone blockers and basically I haven't had a lot of development—so we're debating if I have enough material to work with."[1]

Jennings's case introduces us to a major aspect of gender transition: the use of hormones to achieve the appearance of the opposite sex. Hormones are given to transitioning adults to help them develop secondary sex characteristics of the opposite sex. In children experiencing gender dysphoria, puberty-blocking drugs are sometimes given in order to suppress the normal progression of puberty, thus stopping these children from ever developing secondary sex characteristics common to their natal sex. To understand the issues related to hormone therapy for transgender people, I will review how hormone therapy is used in transgender adults, discuss some risks associated with adult hormone therapy, and then discuss puberty-suppression medications.

HORMONE THERAPY IN TRANSGENDER ADULTS

To understand how hormones are used in gender transition, it is important to see transition as a process with identifiable stages. While there may be variations, the following events are standard parts of the process:

1. The person has a persistent, well-documented desire to be the opposite gender or there is a clinical diagnosis of gender dysphoria. Typically, the endorsements of two qualified physicians or mental health professionals are needed to move forward with hormonal or surgical interventions.

2. The person initiates a public transition and begins dressing and acting like the desired gender for a period of one year, including being addressed by a new name. This "real-life

experience" confirms the desire for surgical transition. Some will find this "real-life experience" disappointing and revert to their birth-sex role.[2]

3. After psychological assessment, the individual begins hormone therapy, with females taking androgens and males taking estrogens.

4. "Top surgery" is a common first surgical step. Females will have double mastectomies to remove their breasts in order to look more masculine. Males will have breast augmentation in order to look more feminine. Some transitioning people do not proceed beyond hormone therapy and top surgery, satisfied with being able to present and pass in public as the desired gender.

5. "Bottom surgery" often follows all of the previous steps. The genitalia are actually surgically rearranged in this surgery or surgeries. Again, many transitioning people never proceed to this stage.

6. Additional cosmetic surgeries include facial surgeries, liposuction, hair removal, and for men, surgery on the vocal chords to give a more feminine-sounding voice. The use of male hormones causes the voices of females to deepen without surgery.

7. Throughout the process, transgender people are encouraged to receive professional counseling to adapt to their new gender identity.[3]

The goals of the gender reassignment process vary from person to person, but the intent is to diminish characteristics of one's natal sex while inducing the characteristics of the opposite sex.[4]

In the transitioning process, hormones may be used as an intervention with no intention of pursuing GRS, or they may be used as part of the process of preparing for GRS. Either way, after a persistent desire to become the other sex is documented, hormone therapy is a first step in the transitioning process. Two major goals of hormone therapy are (1) to reduce the hormone levels of one's biological sex and (2) to replace the natural hormones with those of a person's chosen gender.[5] Sometimes called hormonal gender-affirming therapy, hormonal therapy induces the development of secondary sex characteristics of the new gender and diminishes those of the natal sex. The MtF hormone regimen often includes the use of an antiandrogen (which represses natural male hormones)[6] in conjunction with an estrogen (female hormones), while the FtM regimen only includes androgens (male hormones) and does not require drugs to repress the effects of estrogen. In some cases, natal males use only the antiandrogen in order to reduce masculine characteristics and achieve an androgynous appearance.[7] Hormones may be administered orally or via injections, gels, or patches, but testosterone is usually injected in FtM.[8]

MtF Hormone Therapy

When a male begins taking female hormones, the experience is similar to puberty for a girl (except for the beginning of menstruation). The *Journal of Clinical Endocrinology and Metabolism* lists the effects of cross-hormone treatment in males, how long it takes for the effect to begin, and length of time for the feminizing hormones to reach maximum effect (see table 1).[9]

Hormone therapy also contributes to elimination of body-hair growth, but male facial hair is resistant to hormone therapy, especially in Caucasians.[10] As muscle mass decreases, fat is redistributed and creates a more feminine appearance.

Table 1

Effect	Onset	Maximum
Redistribution of body fat	3–6 months	2–3 years
Decrease in muscle mass	3–6 months	1–2 years
Softening of skin	3–6 months	unknown
Decreased libido	1–3 months	3–6 months
Male sexual dysfunction	variable	variable
Breast growth	3–6 months	2–3 years
Decreased testicular volume	3–6 months	2–3 years[11]
Scalp hair	No regrowth	
Voices changes	None	

FtM Hormone Therapy

Females who take male hormones also go through something similar to puberty for boys. The *Journal of Clinical Endocrinology and Metabolism* lists the effects of cross-hormone treatment in females, along with the length of time for efficacy (see table 2).[12]

Also, females taking cross-sex hormones frequently report an increase in libido. Administration of androgens does not decrease breast size in women. Additionally, some FtM may experience male-pattern baldness, but only if they have the "baldness" gene (which is activated by testosterone). When secondary sex characteristics are satisfactory for the FtM transgender patient, usually after nine to twelve months, testosterone doses are reduced.[13]

Table 2

Effect	Onset	Maximum
Skin oil / acne	1–6 months	1–2 years
Facial/body hair growth	6–12 months	4–5 years[14]
Scalp hair loss	6–12 months	none given
Increased muscle mass	6–12 months	2–5 years
Fat redistribution	1–6 months	2–5 years
Cessation of menses	2–6 months	none given
Clitoral enlargement	3–6 months	1–2 years
Vaginal atrophy	3–6 months	1–2 years
Deepening of voice	6–12 months	1–2 years[15]

Many people report a decrease in subjective feelings of gender dysphoria when they begin hormone therapy and the secondary sex characteristics begin to develop. It is not known if this greater sense of ease is a direct result of the hormones themselves or a derived effect from a lessened libido in MtF or the end of menstruation in FtM. At the same time, not everyone experiencing gender dysphoria wants to use hormonal therapy.

Risks Associated with Hormonal Therapy

The current consensus is that transgender hormone therapy is medically safe, but should be monitored. However, while there is surprisingly little data about the extended use of cross-sex hormones over long periods, transgender hormone treatments also present new health risks to the people using them. The most commonly mentioned clinical concern with hormone treatment for MtF is an increased risk for venous thromboembolism (VTE).[16] This occurs when a blood clot forms in the veins. The VTE can then dislodge and travel via the blood to other parts of the body. If such a blood clot moves to the lungs, it results in a dangerous condition called a pulmonary embolism, a blockage in one of the pulmonary arteries in the lungs. Also, males who develop breasts must begin regular exams for breast cancer, be screened for osteoporosis, and examined for cardiovascular risks associated with estrogen use.

Research indicates that long-term use of hormones may possibly be related in an uncertain manner to higher mortality among MtFs, but not FtMs.[17] A 2011 study discovered that MtFs have a mortality rate 51 percent higher than the general population, while FtMs have no major difference in mortality than the public at large. The higher death rate among MtFs was associated with higher rates of suicide, AIDS, cardiovascular disease, drug abuse, and other unknown causes. No increase was observed in total cancer mortality for MtFs, but lung and hematological cancer mortality rates were elevated. Also, use of female hormones by MtFs was associated with a threefold increased risk of cardiovascular death.[18] While the researchers attributed most of the higher death rate among MtFs to factors beyond using female hormones, there is great uncertainty about the effects of long-term use of cross-sex hormones.

The risks associated with hormone use for FtMs seem to be fewer in number. Clinical problems associated with hormone use for FtM include polycythemia, an increased number of red blood cells in the blood.[19] If the ovaries of an FtM patient are not removed, there is some concern that the use of testosterone could possibly be associated with a higher risk of ovarian cancer.[20]

One area of uncertainty regarding the long-term effects of hormones is the possibility of increased risks for certain cancers. There have been rare reports of breast cancers and prostate carcinomas in MtF transsexuals and rare reports of ovarian carcinoma, breast cancer, and vaginal cancer in FtMs. There have also been some reports of hormone-related tumors in nonreproductive organs in some transsexuals. Though an advocate for

GRS, Louis J. Gooren admits the new era of cross-sex hormones may have effects of which we are yet uncertain, and says, "Risks [for cancer] may become more apparent as subjects age and the duration of hormone exposure increases."[21]

While some effects of hormonal therapy are reversible, several are not. For example, voice changes, facial hair growth, and male-pattern baldness are not reversible for FtMs taking testosterone; but other hormonally induced changes are reversible to varying degrees if hormonal treatment is stopped.[22] In MtFs, breast growth along with development of the nipple-areolar complex are permanent. Furthermore, it is not known if the effects of feminizing hormones on male fertility are reversible.[23]

PUBERTY SUPPRESSION

Puberty is an exciting and terrifying time of life. Our bodies change in ways that are both fascinating and intimidating, all of which is accentuated by a heightened sense of emotions and sensitivity to how we are perceived by others. To make things worse, our concern about how other people think we look emerges at the same time as we develop acne. How maddening! Puberty can be even more terrifying for a child experiencing gender dysphoria. Thus in recent decades some physicians and therapists have suggested that children with gender dysphoria be given drugs to suppress the natural development of puberty in order for the child to determine which gender identity will be embraced at a later time.

Drugs used for puberty suppression are called gonadotrophin-releasing hormone agonists (GnRH agonists). These drugs were originally developed in the early 1980s to help children experiencing "precocious puberty," or puberty at very early ages, such as six or seven, and were merely administered so the child could experience puberty at a more developmentally appropriate age. These drugs, which were developed to address an objectively diagnosable problem, were then used in a different manner when, in 1998, researchers in Holland published an article explaining how the same drugs could be used to postpone normal puberty in kids with gender dysphoria.[24] Males who receive these drugs will not develop any of the secondary sex characteristics associated with puberty such as deepening voice, increase in height, development of body hair, or genital growth. Females taking these drugs will not develop breasts or start their menstrual cycles.

To be effective, the puberty-suppressing drugs have to be administered before the child significantly develops the secondary sex characteristics of his or her biological sex. If a child then chooses later to undergo GRS, the claim is made that the child will achieve a more normal and satisfactory appearance than if he or she had waited until adulthood, when height and body mass are largely fixed. If the child chooses not to transition, the drugs are stopped and puberty then purportedly proceeds as "normal."[25] While puberty suppression is being widely touted by transgender activists,[26] there are numerous concerns associated with the practice.

The first and most obvious concern related to puberty suppression is that the normal process of growth and development is being intentionally stopped. Beyond development of sex characteristics, puberty is also a time when bones grow and our brains mature. What effects will puberty-blocking drugs have on bone development? Transgender advocates are not unaware of this concern. One of the most important professional articles regarding puberty suppression was published in 2006 by authors associated with the Free University of Amsterdam, and it articulated a set of protocols for using puberty-suppressing drugs in children. The authors acknowledged that height would be retarded while children were taking the drugs, so they recommended using "growth-stimulating medication" for girls using the drugs, but didn't seem concerned about the boys' lack of growth. Why? Because they assume these boys will transition to "girls," and having a shorter stature would make them look more feminine.[27] The researchers went on to claim that preliminary data indicated no harm to bone development in the short term, but then admitted, "Long term data on peak bone mass should be assessed before a final conclusion can be drawn."[28] In other words, the researchers are eager to give these children puberty-suppressing drugs, but they are uncertain about the long-term effects on bone density. This is what is known as a *human experiment*.

Beyond bone development, the long-term effects of puberty suppression on brain development are not certain. The same Dutch article from 2006 said, "It is not clear yet how pubertal suppression will influence brain development."[29] This is a startling admission: the researchers are giving children drugs without understanding how this will influence brain development. Again, *they are experimenting on children*. The same Dutch group published a study of adolescents treated with puberty-suppressing drugs, focusing on executive functioning skills of the children, meaning one's ability to manage resources in order to achieve a goal. The report claimed the puberty-suppressing drugs had "no detrimental effects" on executive functioning.[30] However, others who reviewed the findings noted the results of their study, especially for males, were more ambiguous and more suggestive of harm than their optimistic summary indicates.[31]

The large number of cases of gender dysphoria that resolve during adolescence presents another concern with gender-suppression therapy. The *Diagnostic and Statistical Manual of Mental*

Disorders says, "Rates of persistence of gender dysphoria from childhood into adolescence or adulthood vary. In natal males, persistence has ranged from 2.2% to 30%. In natal females, persistence has ranged from 12% to 50%."[32] While these ranges are broad, they indicate that most cases resolve and the children embrace the gender consistent with their natal sex. This is in stark contrast to preliminary data which indicate that the large majority of children who begin puberty suppression eventually decide to continue gender transition.[33] To be clear: Most kids who don't take puberty-suppressing drugs resolve their gender dysphoria; most kids who take puberty-suppressing drugs later transition to the other gender. Why is this so? Perhaps the children being treated have all passed major thresholds in development and would have continued in their gender dysphoria. But Paul Hruz (Washington University School of Medicine), Lawrence Mayer, and Paul R. McHugh (both of Johns Hopkins) addressed the remarkably high number of children receiving puberty suppression who identify as the other gender and offer an important word of warning. They say puberty suppression "may have solidified the feelings of cross-gender identification in these patients, leading them to commit more strongly to sex reassignment than they might have if they had received a different diagnosis or a different course of treatment."[34] It seems the puberty-suppressing drugs don't really provide a time for kids to decide which gender they prefer: instead the drugs push kids toward the opposite gender. Puberty-suppressing drugs are not a neutral therapy; they reinforce transgenderism.

Furthermore, asking a ten-year-old if he or she wants to "suppress puberty" is asking too much of a young child, especially when they have no point of reference for the experience of puberty or the emotional maturity to grasp the second- and third-level consequences of such a choice. For example, one pro-transgender article suggests that children who undergo puberty suppression should demonstrate "a knowledge and understanding of the effects of GnRH, cross-sex hormone treatment, surgery, and the social consequences of sex reassignment."[35] This is asking a child to grasp all the complex and experimental concepts being pushed by adults with avant-garde sexual ethics.

Christians intuitively understand that puberty is a time of vitally important transitions that must be skillfully navigated to arrive spiritually and morally intact at adulthood. In this light, Christians have long known that introducing dangerous variables like drugs, alcohol, or tobacco into a child's life during puberty can have long-term detrimental consequences. These concerns are verified by the extremely negative consequences research has clearly demonstrated take place in the brains of kids who are substance abusers.[36] While puberty-suppressing drugs are not as imminently dangerous as illegal narcotics and the analogy has limits, we should exercise extreme caution when considering stopping the process of puberty altogether. The entire enterprise seems patently unwise, except that the spirit of our age declares we rush forward in redefining gender and human development.

HORMONAL TREATMENT SUMMARY

The use of both cross-sex hormones and puberty-suppressing drugs is a major component of gender reassignment. Neither is without risks, and many changes brought about by the use of cross-sex hormones are irreversible. In the next chapter, we will examine the extreme surgical procedures people undertake in gender reassignment.

KEY POINTS

1. Hormone therapy is a first step in gender transition.

2. The common consensus is that hormonal therapy is medically safe when monitored, but there are side effects and associated risks.

3. Many changes brought about by hormonal therapy are not reversible.

4. Transgender activists urge that children experiencing confusion about gender be given drugs to prevent them from going through puberty.

5. Puberty suppression is not a neutral therapy, but reinforces transgenderism.

CHAPTER 7

GENDER REASSIGNMENT SURGERY

Richard Raskind was a male professional tennis player who underwent gender reassignment surgery (GRS) in 1975 and subsequently competed in professional tennis as the woman Renée Richards. Raskind / Richards commented on the pain involved with GRS in his 1983 biography *Second Serve*, describing the excruciating agony of the surgery as a "bath of suffering" and saying, "It was as if someone was repeatedly poking a firebrand into my groin. Mixed with this was a tearing sensation; it was like someone was ripping at my organs with a pair of pliers."[1] While GRS practices have progressed in the decades since Raskind's / Richards's procedure, it is still a painful and extensive surgical process for both men and women. This chapter will explore this surgical "bath of suffering" and offer a Christian critique of the practice. I will argue that GRS is not a morally acceptable option for Christians experiencing gender dysphoria. To understand this difficult issue, I will begin by

94

briefly discussing why people have GRS, then move to a description of both MtF and FtM GRS, summarize the physical and psychological outcomes of GRS, and conclude with an ethical and theological critique.

In what follows, I will be discussing human genitalia, parts of the body that are private and not generally discussed in public. I realize the awkwardness of discussing such matters, but it is necessary to do so here in order to have a clear understanding of what actually takes place in GRS. Clearly defining the exact procedures in question allows us to offer a robust ethical analysis of whether or not this type of surgery should be performed.

WHY DO PEOPLE HAVE GRS?

GRS is suggested as a way of resolving the conflict caused by gender dysphoria. The idea is that the surgery will bring one's body into alignment with one's psychological sense of gender. In so doing, the hope is that the person will experience less gender dysphoria and attain a state of psychological and emotional well-being. The World Professional Association for Transgender Health (WPATH) says that for some people GRS is "essential and medically necessary" and that "relief from gender dysphoria cannot be achieved without modification of their primary and / or secondary sex characteristics to establish greater congruence with their gender identity."[2] Because of the belief that GRS is therapeutic and corrective, it is sometimes called "gender affirmation surgery."

The ages at which people pursue GRS tend to differ somewhat based on natal sex. Data from the 1990s in the Netherlands indicates that the majority of FtMs apply for reassignment between the ages of twenty and twenty-five, and seldom in middle age. In contrast, the majority of MtFs do so later between the ages of twenty-five and thirty, and middle-aged subjects are not rare.[3] Men consistently ask for GRS more frequently than women.[4] A 2009 study from England had a markedly higher number of males seeking GRS than females and noted an increasing number of people seeking GRS.[5] One reason more males than females seek GRS is related to the fact the MtF surgery is relatively easier to accomplish.

The number of gender reassignment surgeries in the United States is increasing, though most are still just "top" surgeries. The American Society of Plastic Surgeons (ASPS) released its first report on the documented number of GRS in the United States in May 2017, claiming over three thousand such surgeries in 2016.[6] Of these, the majority (54 percent) were on MtF. But in the ASPS data, genital surgery was rare and virtually all of the surgeries recorded were either breast implants for MtF or mastectomies for FtM.[7] The volume of GRSs in the United States is expected to increase, depending on increased coverage by insurance companies, Medicare, and Medicaid.[8]

GRS involves removing a person's original genitalia and fashioning new genital structures that mimic those of the opposite sex. As we saw in the last chapter, gender reassignment is not just one surgery, but is a process involving transitioning one's appearance in clothes and mannerisms ("real-life experience"), hormone therapy, and usually more than one surgery. Some differentiate between the terms "gender reassignment" and "sex reassignment." "Gender reassignment surgery" is used by some authors to refer to all surgical procedures that a patient wishes to receive to resemble the appearance of the opposite gender. As a subset of gender reassignment, "sex reassignment surgery" refers specifically to reconstruction of the genitals.[9] The average person on the street often refers to such surgeries as "sex change surgery." For my purposes, I will simply refer to all procedures as gender reassignment surgery.

TOP SURGERY

"Top surgery" refers to men who receive breast implants in order to look more feminine or women who get mastectomies in order to look more masculine. For many transgender people, top surgery combined with hormonal therapy suffices, and they do not have genital surgery. Top surgery frequently precedes genital surgery.

In MtF, breast augmentation is often a first step after hormonal treatment is begun, with the development of a more feminine profile aiding in the new gender role. Prior to breast augmentation, twelve months of hormone therapy are suggested, as this allows for some breast growth, allowing for better cosmetic results.[10] For some MtFs, the use of feminizing hormones alone provides the desired breast size. Anatomical differences make the outcome of breast augmentation different for males than females, including the wider male chest resulting in breasts being farther apart, more muscle mass in the male chest, and a smaller dimension of the nipple and areola.[11]

FtM transsexuals have their breasts removed in order *not* to look feminine, and will frequently bind their breasts prior to surgery. Different procedures are performed based on the size of breasts involved. Females with smaller breasts may have what is called a subcutaneous mastectomy, where all the breast tissue is removed via an incision. This allows the surgeon to leave the areola and nipple intact. When larger breasts are involved, a breast amputation (double mastectomy) is required, which is a more extensive surgery leaving noticeable scars.[12] To achieve a male-looking result, the nipple and the diameter of the areola are frequently reduced.

MALE-TO-FEMALE GENITAL GENDER REASSIGNMENT SURGERY

The goals of MtF genital GRS are to help a natal male have a female genital appearance and function. To achieve this goal, the testes must be removed (orchiectomy, castration), the penis must be amputated (penectomy), and a labia, clitoris, and vagina must all be created while maintaining good urinary-tract function. Usually, this process takes place in one surgery. Some patients only have cosmetic procedures in which external male genitals are removed, but no vagina is created. In still other cases, men have their sperm collected and stored prior to castration so that they can father children after GRS.

After the penis and testes are removed, a neo-vagina is constructed (vaginoplasty). To do this, a cavity is created between the rectum and prostate (which is not removed), with the goal of creating a vagina ten centimeters in depth and a diameter of thirty millimeters.[13] The major problem in vaginoplasty is finding material to create the neo-vagina. Most commonly, the skin from the penis and/or scrotum is used, with the penile skin being inserted into the new vaginal cavity and attached via skin grafts, a procedure known as "penile inversion." Two British GRS surgeons comment, "In our experience, when the patient is uncircumcised and the penis is of normal adult dimensions, penile skin can be used exclusively for the lining of the vagina."[14] If there is not enough penile skin available, other skin grafts from the hip or buttocks can be used to augment penile skin.[15] Other surgeons use skin taken from the thigh or abdomen to create the new vagina, while still others actually use a section of the colon since the lining of the colon is somewhat similar to the mucous lining of the vagina.[16] Amazingly, even skin taken from inside the cheek has been used to create a vagina in some procedures.[17]

Each vaginoplasty procedure has associated problems. For example, a natal vagina has no hair, but if skin that normally has hair is used to create the neo-vagina, then the skin should be depilated prior to surgery. If not, hair growth in the neo-vagina can be problematic. If tissue from the colon is used, the neo-vagina can have a discharge that is awkward and uncomfortable. Furthermore, the two ends of the colon have to be rejoined after the segment is removed. Use of colon segments is the most common procedure in Iran, though in some Western countries a bowel segment vaginoplasty is used only as a sort of "rescue operation" when skin tube vaginoplasty has failed.[18] In some cases, bisecting the colon to provide an artificial vagina is actually connected to the use of puberty-suppressing drugs. Boys who begin puberty suppression at an early age will sometimes have insufficient penile skin because the penis did not grow normally due to the medication.

In addition to creating a vagina, the urethra must be shortened and relocated in such a way that the direction of the urinary stream is downward in the sitting position. And all this must be done in conjunction with the creation of a neo-clitoris. The sensate skin from the tip of the penis is moved to the location of the clitoris with an accompanying move of the urinary tract. This new clitoris is created by preserving the blood supply along the wall of tissue taken from the penis tip, leaving some of the skin attached to the original site—a procedure called a "pedicle."[19] The topic of ideal reconstruction of the vulva, especially the clitoro-labial complex, is still a field of debate,[20] but usually scrotal skin is used to create an artificial labia. The creation of the vulva and labia are further complicated if scrotal skin had to be used to augment penile skin within the neo-vagina. Reports indicate crafting the labia majora is easier than creating the labia minora.[21]

Regardless of the source of the skin for the neo-vagina, a device has to be inserted to keep it dilated, especially in the early days after surgery. The patient usually stays in bed four to five days, after which the dilator is removed and the person becomes ambulatory. Routine dilation often continues once or twice per week depending on the patient's sexual activity.[22]

FEMALE-TO-MALE GENITAL GENDER REASSIGNMENT SURGERY

The goals of FtM genital gender reassignment surgery are to help a natal female to have a genital appearance and function similar to a natal male. The ability to have penetrative sex, to void while standing, and phallus sensation are often cited as important. GRS is much more challenging for FtMs than MtFs since it is comparatively easier to create an artificial vagina than an artificial penis; therefore, FtM GRS is usually a multistage surgical process. The particulars vary from person to person, but FtM GRS usually includes removal of the ovaries and uterus, sometimes the removal of the vagina, and creation of an artificial scrotum and penis.[23] Some FtMs do not have the vagina removed, but merely closed. Other FtMs forego creation of an artificial penis if the use of male hormones has increased the clitoris size so that it looks like a micro-penis.

Creation of an artificial penis (phalloplasty) is a very difficult process and a technically demanding procedure.[24] So much so, the general consensus seems to be FtM genital reassignment always requires more than one surgery.[25] There is no universal consensus in the way the surgeries proceed. In some cases, FtM genital surgery is performed one year after the patient has had a mastectomy and hysterectomy. The first and most obvious problem is where to find skin to produce the neo-phallus. In the past, a phallus was constructed from a lower abdominal skin flap that was then given a urethra constructed from vaginal epithelium and skin. But the abdominal skin flap is now used less frequently and the use of a radial forearm flap is the most popular approach—meaning skin is taken from the forearm and formed into a phallic shape, then grafted onto the clitoris. In this "forearm" approach, part of the skin is rolled to create a new urethra while the rest is rolled around the new urethra to form a phallus.[26] Other surgeons have stopped trying to create a new urethra in FtM surgery because of the high rate of urological complications.[27]

Perhaps the most difficult and cumbersome aspect of FtM surgery is the fact the artificial phallus cannot achieve an erection. Several remedies have been attempted, such as use of cartilage, bone, rigid implants, or inflatable prosthesis. Usually, such penile implants are surgically put in place about one year after the initial phalloplasty.[28] The results are often awkward imitations and frequently need further surgical attention. FtM GRS often includes the creation of an artificial scrotum. This is generally accomplished by hollowing out the labia majora, and then inserting silicone implants of fake testes.[29]

OUTCOMES OF GRS

What are the outcomes of GRS? Are any deleterious health effects associated with transitioning? Transgender literature frequently mentions that GRS is safe and non-life-threatening, but an evaluation of GRS forces us to recognize that the procedure does not really change one's sex, is irreversible, is associated with some negative outcomes, and has many postoperative difficulties.

GRS Does Not Really Change One's Sex

GRS does not *really* change males into females or vice versa. In fact, the combination of hormone therapy and surgery results in a surgically altered male with high levels of female hormones or a surgically altered female with high levels of testosterone. In 1966, Harry Benjamin, the groundbreaking advocate for GRS, commented on the reality that reassignment surgeries do not change one's sex:

> Medically, or rather endocrinologically, we are reminded that no "female" can ever result from the operations but merely a castrated (or mutilated) male, with artificially created sex organs resembling those of a female and, if successfully created, allowing normal peno-vaginal sex relations. These comments and explanations are naturally correct. Patients are always made aware of them but I have yet to find a transsexual who would be deterred from his goal by these considerations.[30]

Benjamin also said that "these persons [people wanting a sex change], in a strictly scientific sense, fool themselves. No actual change of sex is ever possible." But he quickly added, "Nevertheless, the wish to change sex persists, and for all practical purposes such can and has been accomplished as far as the individual's future life and position in society are concerned."[31]

Many people pursuing GRS can have unrealistic expectations, and the fantasy of changing genders can often exceed the reality of the actual results.[32] We must be clear: An MtF will never ovulate, menstruate, become pregnant, give birth, or nurse a child. An FtM will not have a prostate, will never produce sperm, will never father a child, and none of the surgically created penises function like a natal male's phallus.[33] Furthermore, the person's genetics are still those of his or her birth sex—given a DNA test, an MtF will still show "male" and an FtM will still show "female." Kline and Schrock are quite right when they say, "Complete 'gender reassignment,' or the comprehensive transformation of one sex to the opposite, is impossible."[34]

The terms "sexual reassignment surgery" or "gender reassignment surgery" are quite problematic and imprecise, since the terms assume one is *assigned* a sexual identity at birth and that such an identity can actually be surgically reassigned. But as one group of authors says, "Sexual identity is observed at birth, and, except in rare cases, matches the genetic structure. It is written on every cell of the body and can be determined through DNA testing. It cannot be changed. Calling men who have had [sexual reassignment surgery] 'women' does not change their genetic structure. It does not make them genetic women."[35] Thus, a certain amount of self-deception is involved the GRS process. When Richard Raskind transitioned to become Renée Richards, he commented that in spite of the pain, he felt confident because "I was now a woman."[36] But Raskind was not a woman: He was a man surgically altered to look like a woman.

GRS Is Irreversible

GRS is irreversible: People who have such surgeries have irreparably changed their bodies. While most research indicates that people are satisfied with their GRS,[37] the fact is that some do regret their surgery.[38] But GRS is largely irreversible. For males, testes cannot be reconstructed and, as was seen earlier, a surgically created neophallus has severe limitations. For females, ovaries and a uterus cannot be reconstructed. A 2016 article on surgeries to reverse sex-reassignment surgeries on MtFs made contradictory statements, saying, "Good postoperative results were achieved in all patients," but followed this with, "two patients are currently waiting for penile implants; and one patient decided against the penile prosthesis."[39] It is clear that

the purported good results do not restore the body back to its
original and intact state.

GRS Is Associated with Negative Outcomes

Most reports claim people having GRS do not regret the surgery, but other research indicates a plethora of negative mental
health outcomes associated with GRS. A 2010 article in *Clinical
Endocrinology* reviewed 28 studies involving 1,093 MtF and 801
FtM who underwent GRS. The authors found that 80 percent
reported significant improvement in gender dysphoria, and
78 percent reported significant improvement in psychological
symptoms.[40] But the authors themselves referred to the research
as "very low quality evidence."[41] One study of MtF GRS found
that over 90 percent of patients were satisfied with the aesthetic
result and capacity for orgasm, with 58 percent reporting having
sexual intercourse.[42] At the same time, methodological problems
are common in research on outcomes of GRS, with one source
noting, "Despite many reports of positive outcomes of patients,
there was little consensus of how to measure effectiveness."[43]
The same authors go on to conclude that the research on postoperative satisfaction is flawed and "little robust evidence exists."[44]

Though the data has serious limitations, most studies claim
that people do not regret GRS. But perhaps the more important
question is, Does GRS actually improve a person's psychological
and physical well-being? In a major study from the Karolinska
Institute in Sweden published in 2011, a cohort of 324 sex-re-
assigned people followed over thirty years demonstrated that
numerous problems persisted after reassignment. The authors
concluded, "This study found substantially higher rates of overall mortality, death from cardiovascular disease and suicide,
suicide attempts and psychiatric hospitalizations in sex-reas-
signed transsexual individuals compared to a healthy control

population."[45] The higher mortality rate was primarily due to completed suicides, but death due to cancer and cardiovascular disease was increased as well. Yet in spite of their own data about negative outcomes regarding GRS, the authors still speculate, "Things might have been even worse without sex reassignment."[46] But the most important and robust research regarding GRS strongly indicates that GRS in fact does not resolve underlying issues for many people and the surgery does not bring the hoped-for peace.

Postsurgical Complications

Postoperative problems are common with GRS, with more problems associated with FtM than MtF surgery. One 2009 report on 37 FtMs found that 12 patients had urethral strictures and 6 had a fistula (an abnormal connection between two body parts), and an unnamed number required further corrective surgeries to close the vagina.[47] A group of surgeons specializing in GRS reported that in FtM surgeries "urologic complications were seen in 41 percent of patients (119 of 287), with a fistula in 72, a stricture in 21, and a combination of both in 26."[48] The skin used to create the new urethra is usually taken from hair-bearing skin, and growth of hair within the urethra can cause obstruction to urinary flow.[49] Beyond urological problems, inflatable erectile devices have a limited survival time and often have to be replaced.[50] When all problems are taken into consideration, FtM patients can potentially undergo up to six surgeries within the first year after phalloplasty.[51] The end product remains distinguishable from a natural penis, though the appearance of the neo-phallus has improved as surgical techniques have advanced.[52]

MtF GRS also has common postoperative problems. James Bellringer and Gennaro Selvaggi, both gender reassignment surgeons, say, "By far the most devastating complication of MtF surgery for the patients is the development of a rectal fistula into the neovagina. Finding accurate estimates for the incidence of fistula in the literature is difficult, and the suspicion remains that the complication is seriously under-reported."[53] On other occasions, the new urethral opening will narrow, causing the patient to retain urine and then experience dribbling incontinence, thus requiring further surgery to correct the problem. Postsurgical bleeding is common in MtF GRS, and ruptures along a surgical incision are common, with reports indicating that 10 percent of patients will experience clinically significant levels of bleeding.[54] Beyond these medical problems, the extent to which the person actually experiences erotic sensation in the neovagina is variable.[55]

THEOLOGICAL AND ETHICAL REFLECTION

Ethical and theological critique of GRS shows the procedure fails several tests. GRS violates the ethical principle of "do no harm." It fails a theological critique when examined through the lens of creation, a Christian view regarding our internal thoughts and corresponding desires, and the Christian concept of holiness.

GRS and "First, Do No Harm"

A long-standing principle of Western medical ethics has been, "First, do no harm." Among other things, this means that a physician should not damage a patient or mangle a normal, healthy body. Yet we must be very clear: In GRS, perfectly healthy and functioning urological and reproductive organs are destroyed, removed, and irreversibly transformed and damaged. *Intentional harm is done.* The World Professional Association for Transgender Health is aware of this objection and attempts to respond by saying, "The resistance against performing surgery on the ethical basis of 'above all do no harm' should be respected, discussed, and met with the opportunity to learn from patients themselves about the psychological distress of having gender dysphoria and the potential for harm caused by denying access to appropriate treatments."[56] What is significant about WPATH's response is their unabashed abandonment of nonmaleficence and advocacy of radical moral autonomy. The subjective desires associated with gender dysphoria now trump best practice in medicine for a healthy functioning body. Furthermore, we have seen that GRS is associated with negative mental health outcomes.

Essentially, in GRS a patient is asking to have a perfectly healthy and normally functioning part of his or her body removed. One is reminded of a psychological condition called "body integrity identity disorder," in which a person wants to amputate a perfectly healthy appendage.[57] Surgeons find it unethical to honor a person's request to amputate a healthy limb. Instead, a better plan is to treat the root causes of the psychological distress. Yet, when someone wants to amputate or remove perfectly functioning genitals, the spirit of the times insists that such requests must be honored. If we as a society do not honor a request to amputate a healthy limb, why are we rushing to honor requests to amputate healthy genitalia?

GRS and Creation

As we saw in chapter 3, the gift of gender is an intricate part of being made in the image of God, and Scripture does not differentiate between "sex" and "gender" as separately identifiable concepts. The sex we are given at birth is part of God's will for us as his image-bearers. Furthermore, we are a body-soul unity, with the body and soul connected at all points. These concepts help us understand why Christians should reject GRS as a therapeutic option for gender dysphoria.

An important premise that seems to underlie the request for GRS is a harsh distinction between the soul and body, which is inconsistent with Scripture. People requesting GRS are claiming their internal identity is the "real and good me" imprisoned in a "bad" body of the wrong sex. They are saying, "My body is evil, but my soul is good." But the idea of a "good" soul trapped in an "evil" body has long been rejected by Christians and is inconsistent with Scripture. The ancient heresy of Gnosticism argued the soul was good because it was spiritual, but the body is evil because it is matter. In such systems, the body is somewhat likened to a cage that constrains a good spirit. In this way, the modern claims that "I am a man *trapped* in a woman's body" or "I am a woman *trapped* in a man's body" have strong Gnostic over-tones. To a certain degree, a request for GRS is actually denying the body as one's self, and as Oliver O'Donovan suggests, this reduces the body "to undifferentiated matter, on which the spirit proposes to exercise unlimited freedom."[58]

Our sexual identity as male or female is integral to being made in God's image. If we can learn anything from GRS, perhaps we should learn the degree to which our sexual identity is profoundly related to our bodies. The numerous physical alter-ations a person must endure to transition point us to the amaz-ing complexity of how our sex is an intricate part of our body.[59] In this light, it seems much wiser to find a way to embrace and care for the body God has given us instead of subjecting it to multiple surgeries.

Part of our responsibility as image-bearers is for each of us to be good stewards of the body we are given. Addressing sexual ethics, Paul says in 1 Corinthians 6:19-20, "Or do you not know that your body is a temple of the Holy Spirit who is in you, whom you have from God, and that you are not your own? For you have been bought with a price: therefore glorify God in your body." The idea that we are to glorify God in our bodies has led countless generations of Christians to oppose sexual immorality, gluttony, drunkenness, substance abuse, and a host of other choices and lifestyles destructive to our health and dangerous to our bodies. Our subjective desires for perceived pleasure do not overrule our responsibility to steward the body. Likewise, GRS involves a series of traumatic events to the body, especially the genitals and urinary tract. In GRS, males do not become females and females do not become males; they become mutilated females and males. The autonomous, subjective desire of anticipated pleasure subsequent to GRS does not negate our responsibility to be good stewards of the bodies God has given us.

GRS, Subjective Desires, and Our Inner Thoughts

One is struck by the degree to which GRS is performed based on subjective as opposed to objective criteria. The *APA Handbook of Clinical Psychology* says, "It is currently impossible to diagnose [gender dysphoria] on the basis of objective criteria. Psychologists are therefore dependent on the subjective information given by the person."[60] In other words, a major, traumatic, mutilating procedure is performed based on people's subjective feelings. But can our feelings alone be trusted as a reliable guide for ethical behavior? Scripture strictly warns us about making decisions based solely on subjective feelings, especially when those feelings lead us to choices contrary to God's word.

We are created by God to be creatures who experience emotion, but because of sin our emotions can mislead us in directions far from God. Jeremiah 17:9 says,

The heart is more deceitful than all else
and is desperately sick;
Who can understand it?

Since the heart is incurable and dangerously sick, the emotions that emerge from it are an unreliable guide for ethical decision-making. The heart is a poor moral leader. It must be led. In this light, subjective, emotional desires for GRS should be seen for what they are: a strong deception.

Human emotions are closely related to our thought life. While the Bible does not directly address gender dysphoria, the Bible does offer insights into the way thoughts are connected to subsequent actions. In many ways, our thought life is a preview of coming attractions: What we focus on and think about today drives the choices we make tomorrow. In this light, the desire for GRS is really a battle of thoughts in the mind: One thinks about and imagines becoming the opposite gender. As the thoughts progress, the path to achieve this goal seems rather direct: Have GRS.

Our thought life is strongly influenced by ideas and concepts of the world in which we live. Thus we are reminded in Romans 12:2, "Do not be conformed to this world, but be transformed by the renewing of your mind." We are not to align our thoughts and ethics with the present world in which we live, a world that currently says GRS is a noble and effective path for addressing gender dysphoria. We should be transformed by the renewing of our mind. The purpose of having a renewed mind is found in the second half of Romans 12:2, "So that you may prove what the will of God is, that which is good and acceptable and perfect." The obvious implication is that discernment of God's will is followed by faithful obedience to it.[61]

In any area of sexual morality or integrity regarding gender, an unrestrained thought life can fuel desires to disobey God's commands and ignore God's designs. In this light, the desire for GRS is similar to many other desires common to humanity: People find the idea of being another gender pleasurable, and the more the concept is embraced, the stronger the desire becomes, with each round of fantasy reinforcing erotic pleasure associated with unholy ideas. When fed long enough, such thoughts can seem natural and good. Because our thoughts can be so deceptive, we are admonished to take every thought "captive to the obedience of Christ" (2 Cor 10:5). Every faulty pattern of thought (including a desire for surgical distortion of one's genitalia) should be brought into obedience to Christ.[62]

GRS and Holiness

Subjective emotions and intense, persistent thoughts about being another gender do not serve as sufficient reasons to undergo GRS. Instead, a renewed mind seeks God's will concerning the gift of gender and embraces our natal sex. All of this is part of pursuing Christian holiness. Hebrews 12:14 reminds us, "Strive for peace with everyone, and for the holiness without which no one will see the Lord" (ESV). Jonathan Edwards emphasized that a passion for holiness is a certain sign that one has indeed been converted and is following Christ: holiness "is the highest kind of evidence of the truth of grace to the conscience of the Christian."[63] Edwards also acknowledged that in God's providence he allows trials to come and that such trials "put it to the proof whether men will prefer God to other things in practice."[64] From the perspective of holiness, the impure desire to be the sex opposite to that which we are born, to engage in sexual activity by playing the part of the opposite sex, and to engage in extensive bodily modification to achieve these goals is indeed a temptation and trial and should be resisted by every means at our disposal.

While many people who have had GRS indicate happiness with the results, the process destroys perfectly functioning genitals and urinary tracts, requires extensive reconstruction, is characterized by many postoperative difficulties frequently requiring further corrective surgery, is associated with negative mental health outcomes, violates the ancient principle of "first, do no harm," rejects God's intended plan for the human body, is a decision based on subjective and unreliable feelings, and is inconsistent with a life of holiness.

KEY POINTS

1. GRS does not change someone from one sex to the other.

2. In GRS, perfectly functioning body parts are mutilated and rearranged.

3. Once sexual organs are removed, they cannot be replaced.

4. GRS is inconsistent with Christian ethics.

CHAPTER 8

TRANSGENDERISM AND THE FAMILY

C hristian parents of children experiencing gender dysphoria face a difficult circumstance in today's culture. If parents do not embrace a child's self-declared new gender identity, they are stigmatized as unkind and unloving by advocates of transgenderism. For example, in *Raising the Transgender Child*, Michele Angello and Alisa Bowman strongly argue that parents who do not accept a child's gender diversity are acting against a child's best interest:

> Under the guise of "tough love," other families isolate their children from LGBT peers, remove internet access, control their friendships, and force them to dress in clothing that matches the gender they were assigned at birth. Parents might even drag them to church, where they hear about the sins of cross-gender expression. Or they pray over them, asking God to exorcise the devil from their child to overcome their confusion.

They may even take them to non-mainstream counselors who lay it on thick, telling the children that they will
go to hell if they keep up this "lifestyle."[1]

Angello and Bowman put Christianity in the most negative light,
suggesting all Christians believe kids experiencing gender confusion are demon-possessed or are headed straight to hell. They
criticize parents for controlling a child's internet access, moni-
toring a child's friends, taking them to church, and praying for
them. But certainly the average rational person would agree that
a parent who does these things is establishing healthy boundaries and making decisions in the best interest of the child's
physical, spiritual, and emotional well-being.

There is a genuine concern that, at some point in the future,
transgender activists may attempt to use force of law to determine how parents will care for gender-dysphoric children.
Transgender activist Nicholas Teich comments, "Parents are,
by their nature as adults with decision-making power, some
of the largest obstacles that stand in the way of transgender
kids being able to be their true selves."[2] How do transgender
activists foresee circumventing parents? One tactic is to shame
parents who do not accept and embrace a transgender identity
for their child. For example, the two pro-transgender groups—
GLSEN and the National Center for Transgender Equality—pro-
duced a model transgenderism policy for school districts. The
policy urges schools not to let parents who are not supportive
of a child's transgender identity know that a child goes by a different identity while at school, going so far as to say, "Schools
must create safe and affirming school environments for transgender students, even if the student's family is unsupportive."[3]
In this way, schools are encouraged to view parents who reject
modern, sexually expansive categories as enemies of both the

child and the school. Another tactic would be to use the force of law itself to declare parents who do not embrace their child's transgenderism to be guilty of child abuse, thus making the child a ward of the state. Something very much like this happened in Minnesota in 2016 when Anmarie Calgaro's son was declared an emancipated minor at age fifteen and then began cross-sex hormone therapy without her consent.[4] Although her son now identifies as female, Calgaro still refers to him with male pronouns, prompting transgender activist David Edwards to say, "Purposefully mis-gendering a transgender person is an act of violence. To continually do that to your child is not only insensitive but also really harmful."[5]

How do we as Christian parents navigate these difficult moral waters, especially when confronted with demands that we accept transgenderism in our own child or accept that transgenderism be normalized in school curriculum? If we grant that a transgender identity is inconsistent with being a disciple of Jesus Christ, how do we respond if our own children experience gender dysphoria? What do we do if our adult children "come out" as transgender? A brief attempt to answer these questions will begin by addressing data on childhood gender dysphoria, then address pastoral thoughts for parents of gender-dysphoric children. Next, we will discuss transgenderism and suicide, followed by the difficulties of a child born with a disorder of sexual development. Finally, we will consider what to do if an adult child "comes out."

MOST CASES OF CHILDHOOD GENDER DYSPHORIA RESOLVE

Most children experiencing some level of gender dysphoria will not remain gender dysphoric after puberty, but their dysphoria will resolve. As we saw earlier, according to the *DSM V*, of the natal males who exhibit some level of gender dysphoria, only 2.2 percent to 30 percent of the cases persist into later years.[6] Among natal females, persistence of gender dysphoria ranges between 12 percent and 50 percent.[7] As one can see, the ranges are broad, but Christian psychologist Mark Yarhouse says, "Most cases of gender incongruence in childhood resolve by the time the child reaches adolescence or adulthood."[8] The ages between ten and thirteen seem to be critical for resolution of childhood gender dysphoria,[9] but most parents (though not all) of a child experiencing gender dysphoria can expect the child to embrace his or her natal sex at some point. The more extreme a child's gender dysphoria is, the more closely it seems to be associated with persisting gender dysphoria into later years.[10] Among researchers, there is some debate as to whether children whose gender dysphoria persists and those whose gender dysphoria desists represent two different conditions.[11]

Transgender advocates are critical of claims that most cases of childhood gender dysphoria will self-resolve. For example, *Raising the Transgender Child* includes a chapter titled "It's Not Just a Phase," in which the authors strongly argue that gender dysphoria will usually not resolve. Some of their argumentation is based on the assumption that "transgender kids" have unique brains and are wired differently.[12] But as we have seen, such claims are based on weak evidence. At most what can be said is that in some samples certain variations in the brain correlate with a higher incidence of transgenderism. The crude form of biological determinism assumed by transgender advocates has not been proved.

While gender dysphoria eventually desists for most children, the experience of childhood gender nonconformity is associated with a higher incidence of same-sex attraction in adulthood. While the existing data has wide margins of variability, the *DSM*

V asserts that among children whose gender dysphoria does not persist, between 63 percent and 100 percent of males later report same-sex attraction while between 32 percent and 50 percent of nonpersisting girls report same-sex attraction.[13] In a 2008 report, almost all children whose gender dysphoria continued into later years experienced same-sex attraction while among those whose gender dysphoria did not persist, about half indicated same-sex attraction.[14] A 2011 study on a small group of people reported that all girls in their sample whose gender dysphoria desisted in childhood had a heterosexual orientation as adults, but among the boys whose gender dysphoria desisted, "Two of the boys felt exclusively attracted to boys, three felt attracted to both boys and girls, and one boy reported feeling exclusively attracted to girls."[15] Childhood gender nonconformity does not mean a child will definitely experience same-sex attraction, but the experience is common enough to deserve noting.

PASTORAL THOUGHTS FOR PARENTS OF CHILDREN QUESTIONING THEIR GENDER

What should Christian parents do if their child begins to self-identify as transgender? The advice offered here is pastoral and intended to complement and not replace professional help. Christian parents should love their children, stay calm, reinforce biblical standards, be prepared for criticism from others, and give a firm no to GRS.

First and foremost, love your child while affirming biblical parameters. Never underestimate the power of a parent's unconditional love to help a child navigate the most difficult moral waters. Regardless of the struggles they may experience, all children are a gift from the Lord (Ps 127:3), including children who, for reasons unclear to us, experience gender dysphoria. Jesus loves children (Mark 10:13–16), including children experiencing conflicted thoughts about gender. Regardless of what new challenge a day brings, reaffirm to the child that the old song is true, "Jesus loves me, this I know; for the Bible tells me so." Our love as parents should reflect the love of God described in Romans 5:8: "But God demonstrates His own love toward us, in that while we were yet sinners, Christ died for us." God loved us in spite of our sin and rebellion, and likewise we should love our children even when experiencing the most frustrating attitudes and behaviors. But love *does not mean* we affirm or celebrate every assertion our child makes about sexuality or gender. Biblical love starts with love for God and his design, and then flows toward our children regardless of the brokenness they may feel.

Since most cases of childhood gender dysphoria resolve, parents should stay calm and not panic. Panic can communicate fear, and fear can lead to anxiety in the child and cause fractures in the parent-child relationship. It is common for kids experiencing gender dysphoria to be aware of the incongruence between their internal gender identity and their natal sex at early ages.[16] Such small children are very sensitive to a parent's reaction, so we should resist the temptation to become overly frustrated with every behavior we do not perceive as appropriately masculine or feminine. Angry overreaction never helps any child, and doing so could unnecessarily reinforce feelings of dysphoria. Yarhouse comments, "The boy who loves to cook is not gender dysphoric, but gender identity questions could arise in a context in which his father and peers ridicule him for his interest and relate to him out of rigid stereotypes."[17]

We should teach and affirm the biblical worldview about gender from a young age. People who reject the Bible have more access to our children at earlier ages than any previous generation, and social media is used to connect with children and teenagers experiencing gender dysphoria. Controlling the flow of moral messages to our children now takes a great deal more intentionality and effort. People with a low view of Christian ethics actively pursue children with confused feelings about gender in the hopes of converting them to the world's way of thinking about life, gender, and sex. In other words, we are in spiritual warfare. In such an environment, early messages are the most important, and from a young age we should tell our children, "I'm so glad God made you a girl," or "I'm so glad God made you a boy." We must teach our children that their own bodies should be received with thanksgiving (1 Tim 4:4).[18] Christian parents are right to teach our children that God has designed our bodies for a purpose, and the gift of our birth gender is a part of the goodness of God's creation (Gen 1:26–28).

Recognize that if you choose to affirm biblical ethics concerning sex and gender, you will be criticized by the cultured elite who have disdain for Christian ethics. They frequently resort to name-calling and will call you "transphobic" if you do not embrace your child's claim to transgenderism. All sorts of parents indiscriminately get lumped into the "transphobic" category, from parents who act in an ungodly manner and call their children names and physically abuse them to godly parents who merely affirm that one should embrace his or her natal sex. One secular author insists that parents who don't affirm transgenderism "are still not secure in their own gender authenticity," thus suggesting parents who oppose transgenderism do so because of their own insecurities.[19] The cultured elite will also assume you are ignorant, and thus you need to be educated into a more enlightened approach to gender. As hard as it is, we are still called to love our enemies, even when they are most unkind to us. But love for our enemies does not entail acquiescence to their worldview.

As Christian parents learn to articulate a biblical stance regarding gender, they should learn to examine transgender arguments critically and recognize unstated and unproved assumptions. For example, consider the comments by Teich: "It is easy, and quite common, for parents to pass off their 'daughter's' lifelong masculinity as an extended phase of tomboyishness rather than face the fact that they have actually always had a son rather than a daughter."[20] Notice the false assumption in Teich's comment: A girl who enjoys rough and tumble tomboy behavior is *not really a girl*. In this way, Teich reinforces stereotypes he claims to decry (such as "girls don't play rugby" because being feminine excludes physical exertion). Teich assumes parents of a girl who likes rough-and-tumble play are in some form of denial if they don't see her as transgender, when actually they are making a reasonable and sound conclusion based on human anatomy and God's design.

Finally, be prepared to give a firm no to requests for GRS. In most of the United States, the age of majority when a person can begin making his or her own medical decisions is eighteen. Thus, before treating a patient under the age of eighteen, consent must be obtained from the patient's parent or legal guardian.[21] Parents can and should say no to a child's request for GRS. Such a stance will require a holy "firmness" and an ability to withstand criticism from the child or some health care and mental health professionals. Future developments may include legal provisions for children to circumvent their parents' opposition to GRS. In our most liberal states like California, it is already legal for children to obtain abortions and hormonal contraceptives without parental consent. Christians should not underestimate the degree to which transgender advocates are willing to take children from under the authority of their parents in order to satisfy the transgender agenda.[22]

TRANSGENDERISM, TEENAGERS, AND SUICIDE

The suicide rate among transgender people is remarkably higher than the general population. Data from nonrandom surveys of self-identified transgender people discovered that up to one-third report making one or more suicide attempts in a lifetime, and the attempts occur more frequently among younger transgenders than older ones.[23] The high rate of suicide among transgender teenagers is a common argument used to convince parents to let their child transition. The claim is made that transgender kids are bullied because they don't look like the typical boy or girl. Thus transgender activists contend that letting the teenager transition to the preferred gender will actually eliminate a great deal of bullying, instill a healthy self-image in the child, and help lower suicide rates of transgender teens.

The suicide of seventeen-year-old Joshua Alcorn, who called himself "Leelah," is often cited in arguments that Christian parents should affirm a child's transgender identity. Joshua, who was born male, told his parents he was transgender when he was fourteen. His parents (who are conservative Christians) did not accept his transgender identity, sent him to Christian counseling, took away his phone, and stopped his access to social media. After continuing tension between Joshua and his parents, on December 28, 2014, he killed himself by walking in front of a tractor-trailer on an interstate outside Cincinnati. Joshua had left a suicide note on his Tumblr account in which he blamed his parents and their Christian faith for his death, saying, "The only way I will rest in peace is if one day transgender people aren't treated the way I was. ... My death needs to mean something. My death needs to be counted in the number of transgender people who commit suicide."[24] The Alcorn family has subsequently become the target of angry activists who see Christian parenting as evil.[25]

No parent—Christian or not—wants a child to commit suicide, so how do we respond to this argument? The reasons teenagers commit suicide are often complicated, and the variables at work are even more complex when a child experiences gender dysphoria and then embraces a transgender identity. The common pro-transgender talking point is that parents who affirm a child's natal sex create an unhealthy environment for their transgender teens, which in turn creates such deep internal disharmony that suicide seems to be the only avenue of escape. For many people, loving a child means embracing their transgender identity and helping them transition so they won't commit suicide. In contrast, Christian parents with a high view of Scripture want their child neither to embrace transgenderism nor to commit suicide.

Many disavow the degree to which a culture hostile to faith contributes to suicide and place all blame for suicidal ideation on a religious home life. Secularists tell teenagers they are the result of a mindless process of natural selection and random time and chance, and then the same secular people wonder why children think life has no purpose. Furthermore, children are told the human body has no ultimate, higher goal or use beyond sexual pleasure and self-fulfillment. An endless parade of songs advocates a kind of sexual nihilism with no goal beyond the next bed partner. Yet the same people blame Christians for creating an environment of despair. Perhaps a worldview that says human life has no purpose beyond sexual gratification contributes to the suicide rate of teens in general and transgender teens in particular more than we realize.

No Christian parent wants their child to commit suicide. The brutal truth is that sometimes suicide is manipulative and intended to harm others. This is not to diminish the very real pain, frustration, and even violence that some young people experience when they have confused feelings about gender. Indeed, many kids experiencing gender dysphoria have been bullied in cruel ways, and this is wrong. We want our children to choose the abundant life of Christ (John 10:10) and not to commit suicide, but neither do we want children to set the moral agenda for a family. Ephesians 6:1-4 strikes the right balance between parents and children, saying children are to "obey your parents in the Lord," and then adding, "Fathers, do not provoke your children to anger, but bring them up in the discipline and instruction of the Lord." Harold W. Hoehner, commenting on Ephesians 6:4, says, "Logically, the irritation caused by nagging and demeaning fathers in the context of everyday life may in turn cause children to become angry."[26] Indeed, no parent—especially parents of kids with gender dysphoria—should demean a child by calling him or her names or telling them they are worthless. Instead, we should strive for a tender firmness that embraces God's standards while reaffirming our love for a child and our child's value and purpose.

CHILDREN WITH DSDS

One of the most daunting challenges parents can face is when a child is born with a disorder of sexual development (DSD, a.k.a. intersex), meaning the baby's genitalia are ambiguous in appearance. Recognizing that a baby does not appear typically male or female prompts distress, confusion, and uncertainty.[27] In the past, the standard opinion was the earlier cosmetic surgery on the genitals is done, the better. Often, there was a rush to make the baby look "normal" as soon as possible. Unfortunately, many surgical techniques used to correct the appearance of the child's genitals had very negative outcomes for them as adults, especially with difficulties in sexual intercourse and in normal activities such as tampon use.[28] Modern best practice now suggests the immediate concern for DSD babies is to ensure a good, functional urinary tract and colorectal function while sometimes waiting until a child is older for cosmetic genital reconstruction. Immediate, cosmetic surgery is now recommended for only the most severe cases.[29] These decisions must be made with great care on a case-by-case basis, with the health of the child as the primary concern.

A Christian perspective regarding DSDs is that the gender binary of male and female is the rule, but on rare occasions children face unique challenges regarding sexual development. A DSD should not be considered something shameful: It is a circumstance beyond anyone's control. Instead, parents and medical professionals make the best decision based on the child's unique situation for the gender that best suits them.[30]

In contrast, transgender activists try to take the exceptional cases of DSDs and make them the rule, as if the gender binary were merely a social construction. But building ethical theory on exceptions and not on the general rule is a bad way to do ethics. The Christian approach is more robust: We affirm the gender binary, while making a way to help children with objectively diagnosable DSDs. In a similar way, we affirm the gender binary and find a way to help people who have subjective psychological gender dysphoria, but we do so in a way that affirms identifying with our natal sex. The existence of children with DSDs does not mean we must yield the moral right of way to transgenderism.

AN ADULT CHILD COMES OUT

Christian parents of an adult child who self-identifies as transgender may feel quite confused and discouraged, but there is hope. First, if an adult child comes out as transgender, we should reaffirm that we love them, are praying for them, and do indeed desire the best for their welfare and future. Second, an adult child may accuse his or her parents of many mistakes in child-rearing, especially for failing to accept signs that he or she was transgender at a young age. Parents should openly and freely admit sins of unkindness or failures to create an environment where the lordship of Christ permeates a home. But parents should not apologize or ask for forgiveness for affirming God's gift of gender as the child was growing. Third, we should try our very best to keep communication open with our adult child while graciously opposing transgender identity. Doing so presents the most immediate and perplexing question for most parents: Should I address my child by his or her new identity? If I don't do so, my child has said we will have no further communication. This matter requires an uncommon level of prayer to seek God's will. Some parents will continue to address an adult child by the child's birth name and gender. At the same time, Christians should show mercy to other parents who disagree with transgenderism but address the child by the child's new identity in an effort to reach the child and in hopes of repentance. In some cases, interpersonal dynamics will dictate the best interaction. Finally, never stop praying for your children, regardless of the directions their life choices take them. Christians frequently forget the power of Jesus Christ to change even the most confused life.

SUMMARY

Parenting is the most challenging task any of us can undertake, and the years of puberty and adolescence are full of all sorts of difficulties as our children mature emotionally and sexually. A child experiencing gender dysphoria or a teenager who toys with the idea of transgenderism gives us opportunities to find God's grace and strength. Parents of a child who identifies as transgender should not feel isolated: All of our children have struggles, and children are frequently unhappy when parents set boundaries for appropriate behavior. Every Christian home is composed of parents saved by grace who desperately want our children to be saved by grace and live under the lordship of Jesus Christ. Stand firm and persevere. God's words of encouragement to Paul are true for every parent: "My grace is sufficient for you, for power is perfected in weakness" (2 Cor 12:9 NASB).

KEY POINTS

1. Most cases of childhood gender dysphoria resolve, and the child identifies with his or her natal sex.

2. Parents should unconditionally love their children struggling with gender issues.

3. Parents should establish and maintain wise, biblical standards for children.

4. Transgender teenagers have a high rate of suicide and need special love. This does not mean parents should compromise biblical teachings regarding gender.

CHAPTER 9

TRANSGENDERISM, CHRISTIAN LIVING, AND THE MINISTRY OF THE LOCAL CHURCH

Christopher Beck was a Navy SEAL who retired after twenty years as Senior Chief Petty Officer, having served in numerous combat deployments. Beck is a brave warrior and received the Bronze Star (with Combat Distinguishing Device) and the Purple Heart. Soon after his retirement in 2011, Beck began the process of transitioning to a woman and now identifies as Kristen Beck. Though Beck initially started taking cross-sex hormones, they led to kidney damage, so Beck stopped the hormone treatment and has not had GRS.[1] Concerning worldview beliefs, Beck claims to "yearn for rational thought beyond mere passages from ancient books or bigotry of stereotypes and such. I'm learning to look beyond the many 'labels' that we're forced to abide by in society." Furthermore, Beck says, "Look beyond the label of gender, race, color, religion, age, sexual orientation—or anything. Why can't we just like each other for just being ourselves in all of our diversity as humans? What is wrong with us that we constantly label and judge each other? This inhibits everyone's potential as humans."[2]

Arguments like Beck's often strike a nerve with Christians because our ethics are deeply concerned with mercy and kindness. Furthermore, LGBTQ activists often remind Christians that our Lord Jesus himself showed great mercy to the outcasts of his day. Transgender people then portray themselves as the modern outcasts and conservative Christians as the Pharisees. As such, Christians feel guilty when we are charged with being judgmental. But are LGBTQ activists like Beck right? Are Christian beliefs about gender and sexuality judgmental and an impediment to human progress? Are we merely bigots quoting an outdated Bible?

Transgenderism in many ways is the last phase of the sexual revolution initiated in the 1960s: All sexual boundaries and gender parameters are now abandoned to usher in an era of unrestrained sexual anarchy. Modern transgenderism must be seen as a fundamental dismantling of sexual ethics. Writing in 2004 in *GLQ: A Journal of Gay and Lesbian Studies*, Annamarie Jagose and Don Kulick said, "Of course, the correct relation between sexuality and gender can never be definitively specified. One of the enduring motivations of LGBTQ and feminist scholarship is precisely its inability to pin down that relation or—to put it otherwise—our ceaseless imagining of it in new ways."[3] Indeed, LGBTQ activists are relentlessly pursuing imagining sex and gender in "new ways." In this light, it is not clear if the ever-expanding gender vocabulary is actually describing clinical conditions or creating new categories for sexual exploration. How do we as Christians interact with others in such a cultural environment? In this final chapter, I will summarize the key points about transgenderism and explore ways to remain faithful to a biblical worldview while interacting with transgenderism in our personal lives, our professional careers, and the local church.

GENDER DYSPHORIA VERSUS TRANSGENDER IDENTITY

A Christian stance toward transgenderism will distinguish between someone who experiences gender dysphoria and someone who embraces a transgender identity. Some people experience a very real, subjective sense of gender dysphoria, which is quite distressing for them. It is one thing for someone to acknowledge, "I'm experiencing gender dysphoria and I appreciate your prayers, kindness, and mercy." But it is quite a different thing for someone to say, "I'm transgender, and I'll be adopting a new identity." When someone says, "I experience gender dysphoria," they are merely naming a problem; when someone says, "I am transgender," they are embracing an identity that is inconsistent with Scripture.

NO ONE KNOWS WHAT CAUSES GENDER DYSPHORIA

No one knows what causes gender dysphoria. No one has discovered a transgender gene. No one has discovered a transgender brain. What have been found are some variables that correlate with a higher incidence of transgenderism in certain cases. But no biological or genetic trait has been found that is both necessary and sufficient to cause transgenderism. Thus we should be quite cautious about arguments in favor of transgenderism that attempt to make it a trait like hair color or skin color. At the same time, there is likely a genetic component to transgenderism, much like there is a genetic component to all human behavior. But acknowledging the complex manner in which genetics influence our behavior is far different from claiming some people are predetermined from birth to be transgender.

Some form of the prenatal hormone theory gets the most traction for causing transgenderism, and for many people it has a powerful explanatory appeal. Again, this theory suggests transgenderism arises in the womb from a discrepancy between sexual differentiation of the genitals and sexual differentiation of the brain, thus explaining the experience of feeling like one is trapped in the wrong body. Yet, to date this theory has not been proved. Contradictory claims abound from the several studies of transgender brains. Often, it is not clear if the trait supposedly unique to the transgender brain *preceded* the transgender behavior or if the brain has been changed to a degree by the transgender behavior itself. Furthermore, some research on the brains of transgender people is clouded by the effects of the cross-sex hormones used in transitioning.

At the same time, for many people the experience of gender dysphoria often emerges early in life, is indeed real, causes anxiety and distress, and is a struggle for which the person did not ask. In other cases, gender dysphoria and the accompanying transgenderism are fueled by impure thoughts and sexual practices related to cross-dressing fetishes. Cases in this second category are usually related to gender dysphoria emerging in adulthood.

Since the causes of gender dysphoria are clouded in mystery, a Christian response should always be expressed with a tone of mercy. While this book has focused on the biological and genetic influences suspected in transgenderism, other factors related to dysfunctional homes and childhood abuse are certainly at play in some cases.[4] According to one source, a distinguishing mark of difference between the mental health of transgender people and the general population is the surprisingly high level of emotional neglect during childhood among transgender children.[5] Furthermore, among all people, the age of sexual debut, the context in which it occurred, and the age and gender of the person with whom it occurred all have strong influences on later gender and sexual identity. Considering all these factors, we do not know the painful journeys that lead people to adopt a transgender identity. To add to their confusion, the world has lied to them about the malleability of gender and convinced them their subjective feeling of dysphoria is more important than God's design for the body.

Christians should speak into this chaos with bold, radical love. Our love should be modeled on the love of Jesus Christ, who offered the woman at the well living water so that she would never thirst again (John 4:14), yet confronted her sin with compassionate firmness (John 4:16–18). We will certainly make mistakes as we interact with transgender people, but if we maintain an intimate relationship with Jesus Christ, he will give us guidance concerning necessary course corrections along the way.

GENDER REASSIGNMENT SURGERY IS MORE AKIN TO BODILY MUTILATION

Gender reassignment surgery does not change someone's sex. Instead, males and females surgically mutilate their genitals in order to look like those of the opposite sex, usually with the hope of playing the part of the opposite gender in sexual intercourse. In these surgeries, perfectly functioning urinary tracts are drastically rearranged. The surgery makes a male into a eunuch with mutilated genitalia and gives a woman a body with awkward appendages intended to imitate male genitals. In both cases, perfectly functioning organs are removed based on the subjective desires of the patient. Postoperative problems are common, and even though most patients seem initially satisfied with the basic appearance afterward, there is evidence that the mental health outcomes of postsurgical transgender people are not significantly better than those who do not have the surgery.

PUBERTY IS NOT A DISEASE

Reviewing transgender arguments, one is struck by the degree that puberty is seen as a problem to be avoided. From a Christian perspective, puberty is not a disease, but is a normal process of growth and development and an expected part of the natural maturation into adulthood. Intentionally postponing puberty so a child can determine his or her gender is an ill-conceived attempt of sexually progressive adults to impose their avant-garde agenda on children. A better approach is to love a child experiencing gender dysphoria, walking with him or her through the valley of confusion while affirming the goal of embracing God's design for men and women.

INTERACTING WITH TRANSGENDERISM ON A PERSONAL AND PROFESSIONAL LEVEL

Christians in the fields of medicine, mental health, and education will face some of the most difficult challenges regarding transgenderism. In each of these fields, Christian professionals will encounter standards of care affirming of transgenderism as well as laws demanding that Christians affirm someone's transgender identity. It is clear that deeply held religious beliefs are considered a threat to transgenderism, as transgender activist Nicholas Teich bemoans the "danger" he perceives of people who are not properly indoctrinated in transgender-affirming dogma, saying, "If clinicians have not been taught exactly what to do in a certain situation, then it is common to turn to their own values and morals."[6] Indeed, Christians in many professional arenas will find their own values and morals to be considered dangerous. Of course, a robust and organized defense of the idea that one should embrace his or her natal sex as given by God is certainly the strongest opponent to the transgender ideal.

One of the initial and most daunting challenges Christians face when interacting with a transgender friend or acquaintance is answering this question: How do I address this person? Should I refer to them by their given name or by the name they chose for their transgender identity? What pronouns should I use when addressing this person? For transgender people, this use of language is one of the primary issues, and they are quite insistent on being called by their preferred terms. When we as Christians do not use the name or pronouns preferred by a transgender person, they feel we are delegitimizing their identity. It seems there are perhaps two courses of action for Christians: Refusal to use the new terms of identity or accommodating publicly while not affirming the person's new identity.

Some Christians may adopt what we might call a "nonconformity" stance and refuse to use the new terms of identity for a transgender person. Christians who do so believe, for example, that calling an MtF transgender by a woman's name and using female pronouns is simply lying: The person is not really a female and calling them a female name is participating in the person's lie and enabling him to continue in his illusion of being a woman. Christians who choose such a nonconformity stance will find their greatest challenge at work, and they may be fired for refusing to accommodate. Human resources departments in most corporations are by and large staffed by people who accept the LGBTQ civil rights agenda and, as the bureaucrats writing employee handbooks, use the force of company policy to make others comply. Furthermore, many companies have already restricted religious expression in the workplace, so religiously based objections to a coworker's new transgender identity are not likely to get a friendly hearing. Teachers in particular will face difficulty, as some transgender activists go so far as to argue that teachers should not address the class as "boys and girls," but merely say "students."[7] Christian teachers in public schools who refuse either to use gender-neutral terms or address a child by a new transgender identity are likely to be dismissed as well.

Strengths of the nonconformity stance are that it rightly affirms the creation standards for male and female and demonstrates moral courage in the face of sexual anarchy. A weakness of the stance is that the transgender person will likely receive the refusal to conform as an act of hostility. Christians choosing the nonconformity stance should keep a few questions in mind. First, have I prayed for the person in question and are my actions motivated by love both for the truth and for the person? Second, am I willing to suffer for following my convictions, including loss of employment? Third, if I am dismissed, will I love my enemies and pray for them?

Other Christians may choose a course of action in which they seek to accommodate as much as possible a person's transgender terms of identification while not affirming transgenderism. Strengths of this position might include a desire to keep lines of communication open with a transgender person in hopes of sharing Christ as well as a desire to find a way to remain in an organization in order to be a voice for righteousness. A Christian choosing this course of action should also keep a few questions in mind. First, do I have a clear understanding of the biblical stance on gender, and do I grasp the grievous sin my friend is committing? Second, do I genuinely intend to make an intentional effort to share Christ with this person, given the right time, opportunity, and prompting of the Holy Spirit? Third, am I willing to share my convictions about gender based on Scripture, realizing others in our culture will strongly disagree; or am I looking for a way to avoid the stigma of being a Christian?

There are no easy answers in our culture to the questions posed here, and Christians indeed must be "shrewd as serpents and innocent as doves" (Matt 10:16). I am asking that we as Christians show grace to each other as we try as best as we can to navigate the confusing waters of transgenderism in the public arena. Let's try to think the best of each other, even if we choose to approach our interactions with transgender colleagues differently. Christians who choose the nonconformity stance should be careful not to castigate fellow believers who take a different approach in personal interactions. Christians who choose to accommodate while not compromising convictions should be careful not to call other Christians "Pharisees" who take a nonconformist stance. But if we are going to be faithful to Scripture, the option that is not open to us as Christians is to celebrate a person's gender transition. Furthermore, the tactics we take in the workplace with someone we know casually may be quite different from the approach we take with someone we know quite intimately, such as a family member.

We must seek the guidance of the Holy Spirit to teach us the best way to live under the lordship of Christ in the most difficult circumstances (John 14:26; 16:7). In Luke 12:11–12, Jesus tells his followers that they may be brought before hostile authorities to account for their faith in Christ. In such situations, Jesus reminds us, "The Holy Spirit will teach you in that very hour what you ought to say." Just a few verses earlier, Jesus had said that not even the sparrows are forgotten by God, and then added, "Do not fear; you are more valuable than many sparrows" (Luke 12:8). Much like the persecution Jesus describes in Luke 12, pressure on the issue of transgenderism comes from the raw exercise of power by government or employer that causes one to fear people, not God.[8] The antidote to fear is trust in God's power to keep us, and to have faith in the Holy Spirit to guide us in our interaction with our transgender friends so that God is glorified and we communicate conviction tempered with kindness.

One of the most talked-about subjects regarding transgenderism is bathroom use. Christians are frequently parodied as backward-thinking rubes when we insist people should use the public bathrooms that correspond with their birth sex. Our opponents insist that transgender people have no sexual agenda in using the bathroom and their only purpose is to live in a manner consistent with their subjective sense of gender. Among many problems with this line of argument, the most significant is this: Transgenderism has a broad spectrum of expressions, and it is a long-known fact that some people cross-dress for the purpose of sexual excitement.[9] Our opponents will then argue that I have just described a *transvestite*, and not *transgender*.[10] But the practical distinctions are blurred and not easily discernible regarding public accommodations. A woman has a rational concern not based on unreasoned phobia when a male enters the woman's restroom and should feel no shame in saying so.

TRANSGENDERISM AND THE LOCAL CHURCH

How does a local church interact with the issue of transgenderism? How do we proclaim the gospel to people experiencing gender dysphoria? How should we respond if a cross-dresser or someone who has had GRS comes to church? Three categories of biblical thought can guide our response: temptation, spiritual warfare, and joining conviction with compassion.

As we attempt to develop effective ways in which to relate and minister to transgender people, we should not allow psychological categories to blur clear Christian thinking: We are basically dealing with a temptation to reject God's design and embrace a gender identity separate from one's birth sex. Seen in this light, transgenderism has much in common with all other temptations; mainly, what we feed will grow. Gender dysphoria can be daunting, but the more a person surrenders to cross-gender behavior, the more compelling the desire actually to *be* another gender can become. For example, when Dick Raskind, a.k.a. Renée Richards, started taking cross-gender hormones, he began dressing more frequently as his feminine persona Renée. Raskind / Richards commented on the cascading nature of this change in persona, saying, "What was destructive to one personality was life-giving to the other." He then added, "That which imperiled Dick Raskind strengthened Renée."[11] Indeed, if impure desires are fed, they will be strengthened and eventually dominate our life.

We must be clear that the path of obedience to Christ and the peace he offers is usually not easy and goes contrary to what our flesh says is best. For people experiencing gender dysphoria, the world, the flesh, and the devil all insist that the road to peace and satisfaction is to reject their birth sex and embrace the opposite gender. But Jesus has never promised an easy road; thus he calls us to take up our cross and die to ourselves each day (Mark 8:34). Real love always has boundaries and includes self-sacrifice. As all of us struggle against sin—even some who are tempted to abandon their gender—we discover that his grace is sufficient for each new day. Christians fighting transgender temptation deserve our mercy, since, especially in our current environment, other people will encourage them to embrace transgenderism while fellow Christians may be frightened by someone experiencing this challenge. It is an unenviable position, but the local church exists so we don't have to fight temptation alone.

Christians should not overlook the element of spiritual warfare involved with transgenderism. Ephesians 6:11–12 says, "Put on the full armor of God, so that you will be able to stand firm against the schemes of the devil. For our struggle is not against flesh and blood, but against the rulers, against the powers, against the world forces of this darkness, against the spiritual forces of wickedness in the heavenly places." While the world scoffs at the notion of the devil, the consistent witness of Scripture is that we have a malevolent spiritual enemy who is real and seeks our destruction, both in this life and in the life to come. The word translated "schemes" in Ephesians 6:11 may suggest that the devil has many schemes as opposed to one grand strategy.[12]

It is difficult to know the mysterious schemes in which Satan may use a physical predisposition combined with painful experiences in life and internal confusion to tempt a person toward transgenderism. Yet it is a bit disturbing to read Richard Raskind's description of himself before GRS. Raskind consistently referred to his female alter ego "Renée" in the third person. Before his surgery, Raskind discussed himself "thinking as Renée would think" and said, "Renée refused to die." While dating a girlfriend at Yale, he mentioned that "Renée surfaced twenty times at the most."[13] From a Christian perspective, while not denying the psychological aspects of Richards's experience, it is hard not to see gender dysphoria amplified by evil suggestions from the forces of darkness. It is not my point to conflate all mental health issues with spiritual warfare, nor am I trying to say transgenderism is a case of "demon possession." But to err too far in the other direction and to deny any element of satanic deception in the subject is also dangerous. Jesus himself described Satan as "a liar and the father of lies" (John 8:44). Thus whatever schemes the devil may have, we know they are based on lies. Two areas where Satan consistently deceives people are gender and sexual ethics.

A Christian stance will join conviction about God's creation standard for gender expression with a deep compassion for people experiencing gender dysphoria. It can be quite difficult for most of us to imagine what it feels like to have a desire to be the opposite gender. When we think about the intense pain and the immense amount of complications associated with GRS, someone must be quite desperate indeed if they think such a procedure will end their suffering. Sadly, the best research to date indicates that mental health outcomes do not improve in the long run for postoperative transgender people when compared to transgender people who have never had surgery. We do far better service to people burdened with gender dysphoria to find ways to help them cope with their condition in a manner consistent with God's design as opposed to reordering their bodies via surgery.

Of the many tragedies associated with transgenderism, perhaps what should grieve Christians most is the degree to which many transgender people are searching for love. Research has conclusively shown that transgender people have a consistently higher rate of STDs, especially HIV. In 2007, two researchers interviewed various MtF transgender people at a clinic in San Francisco to determine what factors might be accounting for the unusually high HIV rate among that group. One MtF who called himself Yolanda said, "It's a really hard life. Really hard." Another MtF named Jasmine said, "A lot of us settle. ... I really think that it's so many of us that are getting this [HIV] because we want to be loved." The authors of the article emphasized that Jasmine's description of wanting to be accepted and loved was common to other respondents in the sample.[14] The transparency of these two people is revealing: transgenderism is *really hard*, so hard that someone is willing to endure the scorn of being transgender in a search for inner peace. This gives us some idea of the dysphoria they must feel.

People struggling with transgender temptation are *already loved* by Jesus Christ and are included in the promise of

Romans 5:8: "But God demonstrates His own love toward us, in that while we were yet sinners, Christ died for us." But showing love does not mean the church encourages people to seek gender reassignment. Instead, we walk with people struggling with temptation, patiently praying for strength for each new day and in each new challenge. A local congregation or a denomination that embraces a revisionist handling of Scripture and endorses gender fluidity has dangerously mishandled God's word, which is the most decidedly unloving thing we can ever do for our neighbors or our nation.

What do we do if a person who has already undergone gender transition attends church or comes to faith in Christ? Let us hope that some of our congregations face this problem! The gospel is good news for everyone, and people who have self-identified as transgender are not excluded from the call to repent and believe in Jesus. First, we must be very clear that when a Christian receives Jesus as Lord, that means he is Lord of every aspect of a person's life, including gender and gender expression. Second, our consistent message should be that God's plan is for people to embrace their birth sex. Third, we must emphasize that being a Christ follower means we live a life of repentance. For someone who has altered his or her body through GRS, this means acknowledging the sin of bodily mutilation and rejecting God's design. Genuine repentance will find a way to embrace one's natal sex in an appropriate way.

But, as we encourage people to affirm their natal sex, we must remember that a transgender person who has undergone reassignment has altered his or her body in significant and irreversible ways. Modern attempts to reverse gender reassignment surgery are feeble, and the body will never be the same. Once a person's genitals are removed, no attempt to restore them will ever be the same as the original. Further surgery may place the person at risk for additional complications. Also, health risks are associated with cessation of hormone therapy, and wise counsel will take this into concern as well.[15] Thus, pastoral care will intersect with good medical advice for the most effective way to ensure a person's best physical health considering the irreversible effects of hormonal and surgical treatments. Furthermore, we must keep in mind that data strongly indicate that the use of cross-sex hormones actually alters the brain itself. In short, we must recognize that the process of repentance will be difficult, but the trajectory is still clear—finding an appropriate way to embrace one's natal sex. This will take a great deal of patience and time.

We must also remember that many if not most transgender people have undergone various cosmetic surgeries to achieve a particular appearance, an appearance that is deeper than clothing and/or makeup. A man who has had breast implants and comes to faith in Christ will still have a feminine-looking appearance the next day. Can we be patient with such people, realizing that addressing the many complex changes they have made to their bodies will not happen overnight but will take time? In Acts 8, an Ethiopian eunuch believed on Jesus and was baptized by Philip. In a similar way, modern people who have changed their bodies can also believe on Jesus and be saved. As a resolution adopted by my own denomination says, we should persistently "love our transgender neighbors, seek their good always, welcome them to our churches and, as they repent and believe in Christ, receive them into church membership."[16]

The church should also make every effort to minister to parents of children experiencing gender dysphoria, whether the children are young or are adults. Christian parents of children who self-identify as transgender can feel lonely and isolated in the church. But if we as the church do not love such families, the world will quickly welcome them. While we should never suggest that a transgender identity is acceptable, we can and must walk with parents and families. Too often, the church is quick to blame a child's transgenderism on some failure in the parents when the fact is that in most cases no one knows why a child experiences gender dysphoria. Sometimes churches forget the basic admonition of Ephesians 4:32: "Be kind to one another."

But the church must remember that it is not an act of mercy to enable someone to sin against God. While we acknowledge the brokenness and genuine confusion brought on by gender dysphoria, we should not downplay the radical moral autonomy at the heart of modern transgenderism. In an effort to redefine their own gender, transgender people are simultaneously redefining sexual ethics. In a review of transgender autobiographies, one is struck by the exhibitionist tendencies to tell details of sexual encounters. Transgenderism is not an identity associated with sexual restraint, but is a way of celebrating the rejection of sexual rules. Augustine, commenting on human autonomy, said, "Not to live after the fashion for which he [humanity] was designed is to live a falsehood."[17] Congregations and denominations that affirm transgenderism as an acceptable expression of Christian living have cut themselves loose from the moorings of God's word and are dangerously adrift.

As Christians, our identity is in Christ. In Christ, my old self is crucified (Rom 6:6). In Christ, I am now "clothed ... with Christ" (Gal 3:27). In Christ, my body is a temple of the Holy Spirit (1 Cor 6:19). In Christ, I have died to my old life and my life is now hidden in God (Col 3:3). In Christ, I am a new creation (2 Cor 5:17). In Christ, I am forgiven (Eph 1:7). As Christians, our identity is always *in Christ*. Anything else we embrace as our identity is a false idol competing for worship. Building one's life around a transgender identity is idolatrous. It is the path away from peace and victory.

SUMMARY

Transgenderism is not consistent with a life of Christian discipleship. A robust understanding of Scripture insists we embrace our natal sex and live in accordance with that sex: In other words, to use the secular distinction, we strive to embrace the *gender* consistent with our *sex*. Imitating the opposite sex is strictly forbidden. Likewise, participation in homosexual behavior is sin.

When transgenderism is seen for the confusion it represents, we see clearly that churches should uphold the scriptural gender binary as normative and affirm the truth of Genesis 1:27: The gift of gender is part of the goodness of God's creation. In so doing, we acknowledge that the experience of gender dysphoria is real for many and a burden for which most did not ask. We are reminded of Jesus' words, "Blessed are the merciful, for they shall receive mercy" (Matt 5:7). But from a scriptural perspective, mercy never means we affirm a distortion of God's plan and pretend transgender behavior is morally permissible. Instead, we walk with our brothers and sisters experiencing gender confusion and marshal every resource available to help them overcome this besetting temptation. We pray together, we read Scripture together, we meet for accountability groups, and we grieve together. We seek wise pastoral counsel and engage Christ-honoring mental health professionals to walk through the process of living in congruence with the highest goal in life— the lordship of Jesus Christ for the glory of God. Temptation grows in the dark, but shrivels in the light. When individual churches create an atmosphere that says, "This is a safe place to admit you are tempted to transgender behavior," we can then build the relationships needed to help struggling brothers and sisters walk the long, difficult path to victory. We can accomplish infinitely greater good by affirming the goodness of God's design than by conforming to the spirit of the age.

KEY POINTS

1. No one knows what causes transgenderism.

2. A Christian stance toward transgenderism will distinguish between someone who experiences gender dysphoria as opposed to someone who embraces a transgender identity.

3. Christians can trust God to show them the best way to interact with transgender coworkers and friends.

4. Transgenderism is a very hard life, and transgender people need the love of Jesus Christ.

5. We do not help transgender people by compromising Scripture.

NOTES

Introduction: Transgenderism and Christian Ethics

1. Bruce Jenner, interview by Diane Sawyer, 20/20, April 25, 2015, http://abcnews.go.com/2020/video/bruce-jenner-interview-diane-sawyer-woman-part-30572231.

2. Caitlyn Jenner, Twitter, June 1, 2015, https://twitter.com/Caitlyn_Jenner/status/605407919820013568?ref_src=twsrc%5Etfw.

3. "Caitlyn Jenner Biography," Biography.com, last updated October 5, 2016, http://www.biography.com/people/caitlyn-jenner-307180.

4. As quoted in Vanity Fair, cited in Michelle Tauber et al., "I Am Free: Bruce Jenner Is Now Caitlyn Jenner," People, June 15, 2015, 44.

5. This letter was rescinded by the Trump administration.

6. The bill was replaced in 2017 by another measure.

Chapter 1: The History of Transgenderism

1. Thomas Beatie, Labor of Love: The Story of One Man's Extraordinary Pregnancy (Berkeley, CA: The Seal Press, 2008), 6.

2. This description from Maarten J. Vermaseren, Cybele and Attis: The Myth and the Cult, trans. A. M. H. Lemmers (London: Thames and Hudson, 1977), 97.

3. This description is summarized from Robert Turcan, The Cults of the Roman Empire (Malden, MA: Blackwell, 1992), 45, 49.

4. Magnus Hirschfeld Society, "Institute for Sexual Science (1919–1933)," http://magnus-hirschfeld.de/institute-for-sexual-science-1919-1933/personnel/institute-employees-and-domestic-personnel/ (accessed June 6, 2017).

5. Cited in Joanne Meyerowitz, How Sex Changed: A History of Transsexuality in the United States (Cambridge, MA: Harvard University Press, 2002), 26.

6. Alex Ross, "Berlin Story: How the Germans Invented Gay Rights—More Than a Century Ago," The New Yorker, January 26, 2015, http://www.newyorker.com/magazine/2015/01/26/berlin-story.

7. Vern L. Bullough, "Magnus Hirschfeld: An Often Overlooked Pioneer," Sexuality and Culture 7, no. 1 (2003): 67.

8. Richter's final fate is unknown. He seems to have been lost in the rise of Nazi power.

9. In a favorable review, Vern L. Bullough even said Hirschfeld "did not always distinguish between what he believed and what the existing evidence could demonstrate. When he could not give answers, he fell back on theories that, in the end, proved to be not particularly valid." Bullough, "Magnus Hirschfeld," 69.

10. Richard Elkins, "Science, Politics, and Clinical Intervention: Harry Benjamin, Transsexualism, and the Problem of Heteronormativity," *Sexualities* 8, no. 3 (2005): 306.

11. Much of Benjamin's funding for his work came from wealthy FtM transsexual activist Reed Erickson, born Rita Alma Erickson.

12. This summary of the three types from Vern L. Bullough, *Science in the Bedroom: The History of Sex Research* (New York: Basic Books, 1994), 219–20.

13. Harry Benjamin, *The Transsexual Phenomenon* (New York: Julian Press, 1966), 19.

14. Benjamin, *Transsexual Phenomenon*, 91.

15. Chloe Hadjimatheou, "Christine Jorgensen: 60 Years of Sex Change Ops," *BBC*, November 30, 2012, http://www.bbc.com/news/magazine-20544095.

16. Joanne Meyerowitz, "Transforming Sex: Christine Jorgensen in the Postwar U.S.," *OAH Magazine of History*, March 2006, 19.

17. Greg Levoy, "Transsexuals: Born in the Wrong Body," *Cincinnati Magazine*, November 1984, 147.

18. Walter Frank, *Law and the Gay Rights Story* (New Brunswick, NJ: Rutgers University Press, 2014), 33. Garland was idolized by gay men in that era.

19. Benjamin, *Transsexual Phenomenon*, 3.

20. Robert Stoller, *Sex and Gender: The Development of Masculinity and Femininity* (London: Karnac, 1968), 9–10.

21. Allen Ginsburg, cited in Timothy Miller, *The Hippies and American Values* (Knoxville: University of Tennessee Press, 1991), 93n31.

22. Ronald Nash, *Life's Ultimate Questions: An introduction to Philosophy* (Grand Rapids: Zondervan, 1999), 204.

23. Holiday Simmons and Fresh! White, "Our Many Selves," in *Trans Bodies Trans Selves: A Resource for the Transgender Community*, ed. Laura Erickson-Schroth (Oxford: Oxford University Press, 2014), 3.

24. Simmons and White, "Our Many Selves," 3.

25. Simmons and White, "Our Many Selves," 9.

26. My comments here are influenced by Albert Mohler, address to the research fellows of the Ethics and Religious Liberties Commission (ERLC), August 30, 2017, personal notes.

27. David E. Garland, *Colossians/Philemon*, NIV Application Commentary (Grand Rapids: Zondervan, 1998), 205.

Chapter 2: The Vocabulary of Transgenderism

1. Lindsay Collin, Michael Goodman, and Vin Tangpricha, "Worldwide Prevalence of Transgender and Gender Non-conformity," in *Principles of Transgender Medicine and Surgery*, ed. Randi Ettner, Stan Monstrey, and Eli Coleman, 2nd ed. (New York: Routledge, 2016), 16.

2. M. Landé, J. Walinder, and B. Lundström, "Incidence and Sex Ratio of Transsexualism in Sweden," *Acta Psychiatrica Scandinavica* 93, no. 4 (1996): 261–63. Data gathered in the 1990s calculated the prevalence of transsexualism in The Netherlands as 1:11,900 males and 1:30,400 females. P. J. van Kesteren, L. J. Gooren, and J. A. Megens, "An Epidemiological and Demographic Study of Transsexuals in the Netherlands," *Archives of Sexual Behavior* 25, no.6 (1996): 589–600.

3. A. Michel, C. Mormont, and J. J. Legros, "A Psychoendocrinological Overview of Transsexualism," *European Journal of Endocrinology* 145 (2001): 365–76.

4. Andrew R. Flores et al., "How Many Adults Identify as Transgender in the United States?," The Williams Institute, June 2016, https://williamsinstitute .law.ucla.edu/wp-content/uploads/How-Many-Adults-Identify-as-Transgender -in-the-United-States.pdf.

5. Jody Herman et al., "Age of Individuals Who Identify as Transgender in the United States," The Williams Institute, January 2017, 2, http:// williamsinstitute.law.ucla.edu/wp-content/uploads/TransAgeReport.pdf.

6. Vaughn Roberts, *Transgender: A Talking Points Book* (Purcellville, VA: The Good Book Company, 2016), 19.

7. Mark Yarhouse, *Understanding Gender Dysphoria: Navigating Transgender Issues in a Changing Culture* (Downers Grove, IL: IVP Academic, 2015), 17.

8. Robert J. Stoller, *Sex and Gender: The Development of Masculinity and Femininity*, Maresfield Library (London: Karnac, 1968), 10.

9. American Psychological Association, "Answers to Your Questions about Transgender People, Gender Identity, and Gender Expression," 2014, 1, http:// www.apa.org/topics/lgbt/transgender.pdf.

10. Rylan Jay Testa, Deborah Coolhart, and Jayme Peta, *The Gender Quest Workbook* (Oakland, CA: Instant Help Books, 2015), 12. See also Fred A. Bernstein, "On Campus, Rethinking Biology 101," *New York Times*, March 7, 2004, http://www .nytimes.com/2004/03/07/style/on-campus-rethinking-biology-101.html.

11. Nicolas M. Teich, *Transgender 101: A Simple Guide to a Complex Issue* (New York; Columbia University Press, 2012), 2.

12. This definition is combined from Teich, *Transgender 101*, 3; Yarhouse, *Understanding Gender Dysphoria*, 20; Heather Looy and Hessel Bouma III, "The Nature of Gender: Gender Identity in Persons Who Are Intersexed or Transgendered," *Journal of Psychology and Theology* 33 (2005): 168.

13. Gennaro Selvaggi et al., "Gender Identity Disorder: General Overview and Surgical Treatment for Vaginoplasty in Male-to-Female Transsexuals," *Plastic and Reconstructive Surgery* 116, no. 6 (2005): 136.

14. See Yarhouse, *Understanding Gender Dysphoria*, 74. This form is called auto-gynephilia. See A. A. Lawrence, "Autogynephilia: An Unappreciated Paraphilia," *Advances in Pscyhosomatic Medicine* 31 (2011): 135–48. The theory is not without detractors.

15. Laura Erickson-Schroth, "Update on the Biology of Transgender Identity," *Journal of Gay and Lesbian Mental Health* 17 (2013): 151.

16. Volkmar Sigusch, "The Neosexual Revolution," *Archives of Sexual Behavior* 27, no. 4 (1998): 331.

17. Matt Huston, "None of the Above: An Emerging Group of Transgender People Is Looking Beyond 'Man' and 'Woman,'" *Psychology Today*, March 1, 2015, 30.

18. Bojan Koltaj, "Queer(ing) Zizek," in *Queering Paradigms VI: Interventions, Ethics, and Glocalities*, ed. Bee Scherer (Oxford: Peter Lang, 2016), 27.

19. Teich, *Transgender 101*, 17.

20. American Psychological Association, "Answers to Your Questions," 2.

21. Huston, "None of the Above," 30.

22. Peggy T. Cohen-Kettenis and Thomas D. Steensma, "Gender Dysphoria," in *APA Handbook of Clinical Psychology*, vol. 4, *Psychopathology and Health*, ed. John C. Norcross et al. (Washington, DC: American Psychological Association, 2016), 395.

23. "Resources on Gender-Expansive Children and Youth," Human Rights Campaign, http://www.hrc.org/resources/resources-on-gender-expansive -children-and-youth.

24. Diane Ehrensaft, "Boys Will Be Girls, Girls Will Be Boys: Children Affect Parents as Parents Affect Children in Gender Nonconformity," *Psychoanalytic Psychology* 28, no. 4 (2011): 529.

25. *Diagnostic and Statistical Manual of Mental Disorders V* (Arlington, VA: American Psychiatric Association, 2013), 452–53.

26. Yarhouse, *Understanding Gender Dysphoria*, 20.

27. *Diagnostic and Statistical Manual of Mental Disorders* (Washington, DC: American Psychiatric Association Mental Hospital Service, 1952), 39.

28. *Diagnostical and Statistical Manual of Mental Disorders II* (Washington, DC: American Psychiatric Association, 1968), 44.

29. For more information about the change in the *DSM II*, see my discussion in *Born This Way? Homosexuality, Science, and the Scriptures* (Wooster, OH: Weaver, 2016), 31–40.

30. *Diagnostic and Statistical Manual of Mental Disorders III* (Washington, DC: The American Psychiatric Association, 1980), 261.

31. *DSM III*, 262.

32. *Diagnostic and Statistical Manual of Mental Disorders IV–TR* (Washington, DC: American Psychiatric Association, 2000), 577. Teich says transsexualism was "replaced" by Gender Identity Disorder in 1994, but this is imprecise since GID was already mentioned in the *DSM III*. Perhaps it is more accurate to say transsexualism was eliminated in 1994 and all such issues were simply called GID in the *DSM IV*. See Teich, *Transgender 101*, 79–80.

33. *DSM IV–TR*, 574–75.

34. *DSM V*, 452.

35. See Teich, *Transgender 101*, 84.

36. *DSM V*, 453.

37. Regarding the relationship of Christianity to psychiatry and psychology, I favor an integrational stance as opposed to other Christians who favor a nouthetic approach.

38. Teich, *Transgenderism 101*, 86.

39. American Psychological Association, "Answers to Your Questions," 3.

40. Kevan Wylie et al., "Good Practice Guidelines for the Assessment and Treatment of Adults with Gender Dysphoria," *Sexual Relationship Therapy* 29, no. 2 (2014): 166.

41. American Psychological Association, "Guidelines for Psychological Practice with Transgender and Gender Nonconforming People," *American Psychologist* 70, no. 9 (2015): 835.

42. Theodore R. Burnes et al., "Competencies for Counseling Transgender Clients," Association for Lesbian, Gay, Bisexual, and Transgender Issues in Counseling, November 7, 2009, https://www.counseling.org/Resources/Competencies/ALGBTIC_Competencies.pdf.

43. Gennaro Selvaggi and James Bellringer, "Gender Reassignment Surgery: An Overview," *Nature Review of Urology* 8, no. 5 (2011): 275.

44. In the early literature, David was referred to by the pseudonyms "John" and "Joan."

45. John Money and Anke A. Ehrhardt, *Man and Woman, Boy and Girl* (Baltimore: Johns Hopkins University Press, 1972), 144–45.

46. Milton Diamond and H. Keith Sigmundson, "Sex-Reassignment at Birth: Long-Term Review and Clinical Implications," *Archives of Pediatrics and Adolescent Medicine* 151, no. 3 (1997): 298–304.

47. John Colapinto, *As Nature Made Him: The Boy Who Was Raised as a Girl* (New York: HarperCollins, 2001), 98.

48. Colapinto, *As Nature Made Him*, 87.

49. Patricia Gherovici, *Please Select Your Gender* (New York: Routledge, 2010), 137.

50. Ritch C. Savin-Williams, "The New Sexual Minority Teenager: Freedom from Traditional Notions of Sexual Identity," in *The Meaning of Sexual Identity in the Twenty-First Century*, ed. Judith S. Kaufman and David A. Powell (Newcastle Upon Tyne, UK: Cambridge Scholars, 2014), 9.

Chapter 3: Scripture and Transgenderism

1. Bob Allen, "Transgender Baptist Minister Depends on 'Theology of Survival,'" *Baptist News Global*, April 11, 2016, http://baptistnews.com/article/transgender-baptist-minister-depends-on-theology-of-survival/#.Wfl_KHZOnIU.

2. I am distinguishing my stance from that of Christian psychologist Mark Yarhouse, who says Scripture is "an important *resource* in any discussion about matters of life and faith and ministry." *Understanding Gender Dysphoria* (Downers Grove, IL: IVP Academic, 2015), 29 (emphasis added).

3. Yarhouse's book is weak in that his chapter "A Christian Perspective on Gender Dysphoria" omits any significant discussion of the creation narrative. See *Understanding Gender Dysphoria*, 29–60.

4. It is too restrictive to limit the meaning of the Hebrew word for "kind" to "species." Victor Hamilton, *The Book of Genesis Chapters 1–17*, New International Commentary on the Old Testament (Grand Rapids: Eerdmans, 1990), 126. Walter Kaiser, commenting on the Hebrew word *min*, says, "God created the basic forms of life called *min* which can be classified according to modern biologists and zoologists as sometimes species, sometimes genus, sometimes family or order." Walter C. Kaiser Jr., "*Min*, Kind," in *Theological Wordbook of the Old Testament*, ed. R. Laird Harris, Gleason Archer, and Bruce Waltke (Chicago: Moody Press, 1980), 1:503–4.

5. I am suggesting God has shared his communicable attributes via the image of God, while his incommunicable attributes are retained for himself.

6. Allen P. Ross, *Creation and Blessing: A Guide to the Study and Exposition of Genesis* (Grand Rapids: Baker, 1998), 112.

7. Wayne Grudem, *Systematic Theology* (Grand Rapids: Zondervan, 1994), 473. I recognize the Hebrew word *nephesh* is broad in meaning and can even be used in reference to animals (Gen 1:21). But debates about *nephesh* seem to miss

the thrust of Genesis 2:7: God gave Adam life personally and directly, and the biblical trajectory is that his life is a body-soul unity.

8. Millard Erickson calls this view "conditional unity." See Millard Erickson, *Christian Theology*, 2nd ed. (Grand Rapids: Baker, 1998), 554–57.

9. Hamilton, *Genesis 1–17*, 139.

10. My thoughts here are influenced by John Calvin, *A Commentary on Genesis*, trans. John King (Edinburgh: Banner of Truth Trust, 1965), 132–33.

11. Daniel I. Block, *Deuteronomy*, NIV Application Commentary (Grand Rapids: Zondervan, 2012), 512.

12. Michael A. Grisanti, "*t'b*," in *New International Dictionary of Old Testament Theology and Exegesis*, ed. Willem A. VanGemeren (Grand Rapids: Zondervan, 1997), 4:316.

13. Nili Sacher Fox, "Gender Transformation and Transgression: Contextualizing the Prohibition of Cross-Dressing in Deuteronomy 22:5," in *Mishneb Todah: Studies in Deuteronomy and Its Cultural Context in Honor of Jeffrey H. Tigay*, ed. Nili Sacher Fox, D. A. Glat-Gilad, and M. J. Williams (Winona Lake, IN: Eisenbrauns, 2009), 51.

14. Fox, "Gender Transformation and Transgression ,"512.

15. Kaiser, *Toward Old Testament Ethics*, 198.

16. "Erra and Ishum," trans. Stephanie Dalley, in *The Context of Scripture*, ed. William W. Hallo (Leiden: Brill, 1997), 1:413.

17. Block, *Deuteronomy*, 534n3. Eugene Merrill suggests a more generic interpretation and says either destruction of the testicles or castration of the penis "may, presumably, be genetic, accidental, or intentional; but that is irrelevant because the end result is the same—the male thus deformed could have no access to the assembly of the Lord." Eugene Merrill, *Deuteronomy*, New American Commentary 4 (Nashville: Broadman & Holman, 1994), 307.

18. N. Allan Moseley, *Thinking against the Grain: Developing a Biblical Worldview in a Culture of Myths* (Grand Rapids: Kregel, 2003), 52.

19. I also contend the importance of gender-appropriate behavior is seen in 1 Corinthians 11:6: "For if a woman does not cover her head, let her also have her hair cut off; but if it is disgraceful for a woman to have her hair cut off or her head shaved, let her cover her head." While I recognize the uncertain nature and extended debate about the passage, I suggest the women at Corinth may have confused Christian equality between men and women with the wrongheaded idea that gender roles and gender identities were now abolished and shaved their head as a signal that gender distinctions are abolished. But Paul calls a woman with a shaved head a disgrace and shame, insisting she was fundamentally rejecting her God-ordained gender identity. Nonetheless, this text is not central to my critique of transgenderism. See Anthony C. Thiselton, *The First Epistle to the Corinthians*, New International Greek Testament Commentary (Grand Rapids: Eerdmans, 2000), 829–30.

20. Nolland suggests this is somewhat equivalent to our modern categories of intersex / DSDs. He comments, "As now, children were occasionally born with defective genitals and subsequently would fail to develop male secondary characteristics as they grew up." John Nolland, *The Gospel of Matthew*, New International Greek Testament Commentary (Grand Rapids: Eerdmans, 2005), 778.

21. See Gilbert Herdt, "Introduction: Third Sexes and Gender," in *Third Sex, Third Gender: Beyond Sexual Dimorphism in Culture and History*, ed. Gilbert Herdt (New York: Zone, 1993), 48.

22. Thomas K. Hubbard, *Homosexuality in Greece and Rome: A Sourcebook of Basic Documents* (Berkeley: University of California Press, 2003), 346.

23. Nigel Rodgers, *Roman Empire* (New York: Metro Books, 2008), 495.

24. Frederick W. Danker, Walter Bauer, William F. Arndt, and F. Wilbur Gingrich, eds., *A Greek-English Lexicon of the New Testament and Other Early Christian Literature*, 3rd ed. (Chicago: University of Chicago Press, 2000), s.v. μαλακός.

25. Danker, *Greek-English Lexicon*, s.v. ἀρσενοκοίτης. The lexicon gives the basic definition of "a male who engages in sexual activity with a person of his own sex," but then adds that when it is paired with μαλακός, it means "one who assumes the dominant role in same-sex activity."

26. I recognize the extensive debate regarding these terms. For a defense of my stance, see David Garland, *1 Corinthians*, Baker Exegetical Commentary on the New Testament (Grand Rapids: Baker Academic, 2003), 211–15; Robert Gagnon, *The Bible and Homosexual Practice* (Nashville: Abingdon, 2001), 303–36.

27. Richard Baxter, *The Reformed Pastor*, ed. William Brown (Edinburgh: Banner of Truth Trust, 1974), 56.

28. *The Baptist Faith and Message*, Article III, "Man."

29. Gagnon, *Bible and Homosexual Practice*, 451.

30. A. Garcia-Falqueras and Dick Swaab, "Sexual Hormones and the Brain: An Essential Alliance for Sexual Identity and Sexual Orientation," *Endocrine Development* 17 (2010): 22.

31. W. Harold Mare, *1 Corinthians*, Expositor's Bible Commentary 10 (Grand Rapids: Zondervan, 1976), 226.

32. Nicholas M. Teich, *Transgender 101: A Simple Guide to a Complex Issue* (New York: Columbia University Press, 2012), 99.

Chapter 4: Genetics and Transgenderism

1. Stefani Germanotta, "Born This Way," track 2 on Lady Gaga, *Born This Way*, Interscope Records, 2011.

2. For a summary of the theory, see A. Mansouri, K. Kosidou, and I. Savic, "Anatomical and Functional Findings in Female-to-Male Transsexuals: Testing a New Hypothesis," *Cerebral Cortex* 27, no. 2 (2017): 998–1010. An early description of the theory is found in G. Dörner et al., "Gene- and Environment-Dependent Neuroendocrine Etiogenesis of Homosexuality and Transsexualism," *Experimental and Clinical Endocrinology* 98, no. 2 (1991): 141–50.

3. National Institutes of Health, "Is Eye Color Determined by Genetics?," Genetics Home Reference, June 5, 2018, https://ghr.nlm.nih.gov/primer/traits/eyecolor.

4. "Understanding Hormone Receptors and What They Do," Breastcancer.org, January 26, 2017, http://www.breastcancer.org/symptoms/diagnosis/hormone_status/understanding.

5. Androgens (like testosterone) bind to the androgen receptors in a cell's nucleus, which tells certain genes to "go to work," especially during puberty. Estrogen binds to estrogen receptors in the nucleus, affecting the important

genes in sexual development. Wenqing Gao, Casey E. Bohl, and James T. Dalton, "Chemistry and Structural Biology of Androgen Receptor," *Chemical Reviews* 105, no. 9 (2005): 3352.

6. Susanne Henningsson et al., "Sex Steroid-Related Genes and Male-to-Female Transsexualism," *Psychoneuroendocrinology* 30 (2005): 663. Their sample included 229 controls.

7. Henningsson et al., "Sex Steroid-Related Genes," 661–62.

8. Lauren Hare et al., "Androgen Receptor Repeat Length Polymorphism Associated with Male-to-Female Transsexualism," *Biological Psychiatry* 65, no. 1 (2009): 93–96. The authors suggest, "It is possible that a decrease in testosterone levels in the brain during development might result in incomplete masculinization of the brain in male-to-female transsexuals, resulting in a more feminized brain and a female gender identity."

9. H. Ujike et al., "Association Study of Gender Identity Disorder and Sex-Hormone Related Genes," *Progress In Neuro-Psychopharmacology and Biological Psychiatry* 33, no. 7 (2009): 1241. They also suggest that the differences in their findings may be due to using an Asian versus Caucasian sample.

10. Rosa Fernandez et al., "Association of ERBeta, AR, and CYP19A1 Genes and MtF transsexualism," *Journal of Sexual Medicine* 11, no. 12 (2014): 2986–94; Rosa Fernandez et al., "The (CA)n Polymorphism of ERBeta Gene Is Associated With FtM Transsexualism," *Journal of Sexual Medicine* 11, no. 3 (2014): 720–28. Of some interest, when the researchers applied the binary logistic regression model, none of the interactions were statistically significant.

11. E. K. Bentz et al., "A Polymorphism of the CYP17 Gene Related to Sex Steroid Metabolism Is Associated with Female-to-Male but Not Male-to-Female Transsexualism," *Fertility and Sterility* 90, no. 1 (2008): 56–59.

12. Rosa Fernández et al., "The CYP17 MspA1 Polymorphism and the Gender Dysphoria," *Journal of Sexual Medicine* 12, no. 6 (2015): 1332.

13. Rosa Fernández et al., "The CYP17-MspA1 rs743572 Polymorphism Is Not Associated with Gender Dysphoria," *Genes and Genomics* 38, no. 12 (2016): 1145–50.

14. National Institutes of Health, "SRD5A2 Gene," Genetics Home Reference, US National Library of Medicine, July 5, 2017, https://ghr.nlm.nih.gov/gene/SRD5A2.

15. Eva-Katrin Bentz et al., "A Common Polymorphism of the SRD5A2 Gene and Transsexualism," *Reproductive Sciences* 14, no. 7 (2007): 708.

16. E. Gómez-Gil et al., "Familiality of Gender Identity Disorder In Non-Twin Siblings," *Archives of Sexual Behavior* 39, no. 2 (2010): 546–52. See also detailing R. Green, "Family Occurrence of 'Gender Dysphoria': Ten Sibling or Parent-Child Pairs," *Archives of Sexual Behavior* 29, no. 5 (2000): 499–507.

17. Richard Green, "Gender Development and Reassignment," *Psychiatry* 6, no. 3 (2007): 121. Green does suggest some transsexuals have a dearth of uncles on their mothers' side.

18. Laura Erickson-Schroth, "Update on the Biology of Transgender Identity," *Journal of Gay and Lesbian Mental Health* 17, no. 2 (2013): 153.

19. A. Burri et al., "Genetic and Environmental Influences on Female Sexual Orientation, Childhood Gender Typicality, and Adult Gender Identity," *PLoS One* 6 (July 7, 2011): http://journals.plos.org/plosone/article?id=10.1371/journal.pone.0021982.

20. Gunter Heylens et al., "Gender Identity Disorder in Twins: A Review of the Case Report Literature," *Journal of Sexual Medicine* 9, no. 3 (2012): 751-57. The authors say their findings suggest a role for genetic factors in the development of gender identity disorder. While these findings are intriguing, the sample is derived from various case studies and it is difficult to know the degree to which it is representative; thus the authors may overestimate the genetic influence on transgenderism.

21. Daniel Klink and Martin Den Jeijer, "Genetic Aspects of Gender Identity Development and Gender Dysphoria," in *Gender Dysphoria and Disorders of Sexual Development: Progress in Care and Knowledge*, ed. B. P. C. Kreukels et al. (New York: Springer Science & Business, 2014), 37.

22. "Study Finds Epigenetics, Not Genetics, Underlies Homosexuality," National Institute for Mathematical and Biological Synthesis, December 11, 2012, http://www.nimbios.org/press/FS_homosexuality.

23. Nessa Carey, *The Epigenetics Revolution: How Modern Biology Is Rewriting Our Understanding of Genetics, Disease, and Inheritance* (New York: Columbia University Press, 2012), 55.

24. Carey, *Epigenetics Revolution*, 55.

25. R. Green and E. B. Keverne, "The Disparate Maternal Aunt-Uncle Ratio in Male Transsexuals: An Explanation Invoking Genomic Imprinting," *Journal of Theoretical Biology* 202 (January 7, 2000): 55-63.

26. Thomas E. Bevan, *The Psychobiology of Transsexualism and Transgenderism: A New View Based on Scientific Evidence* (Santa Barbara, CA: Praeger, 2015), 102.

27. Klink and Den Jeijer, "Genetic Aspects," 45.

28. For a summary of the findings on alcoholism and epigenetics, see Harish R. Krishnan et al., "The Epigenetic Landscape of Alcoholism," *International Review of Neurobiology* 115 (2014): 75-116.

29. We should be open to the possibility that use of cross-sex hormones can alter the epigenetic structures related to both androgen and estrogen receptors.

30. Laura Erickson-Schroth, "Update on the Biology of Transgender Identity," *Journal of Gay and Lesbian Mental Health* 17 (2013): 154.

31. Erickson-Schroth, "Update," 155.

32. Bevan, *Psychobiology of Transsexualism*, 182.

Chapter 5: The Brain and Transgenderism

1. "Chaz Bono: I Was Born a Man," *Fox News*, May 10, 2011, http://www.foxnews.com/entertainment/2011/05/10/chaz-bono-born-man.html.

2. A provocative 2015 article claims that human brains cannot be categorized into two distinct sexes. Daphne Joel et al., "Sex Beyond the Genitalia: The Human Brain Mosaic," *Proceedings of the National Academy of Sciences* 112, no. 50 (2015): 15468-73.

3. One work says, "Perhaps the most reliable conclusion we can draw about sexual dimorphisms in human brain structure is that there are so few of them." Mark Bear, Barry W. Connors, and Michael A. Paradiso, *Neuroscience: Exploring the Brain*, 3rd ed. (Baltimore: Lippincott, Williams, and Wilkins, 2007), 546, 548.

4. Amber N. V. Ruigrok et al., "A Meta-analysis of Sex Differences in Human Brain Structure," *Neuroscience and Behavioral Reviews* 39 (2014): 37.

5. Ruben C. Gur et al., "Sex Differences in Brain Gray and White Matter in Healthy Young Adults: Correlations With Cognitive Performance," *Journal of Neuroscience* 19, no. 10 (1999): 4065.

6. Stephan Hamann, "Sex Differences in the Responses of the Human Amygdala," *The Neuroscientist* 11, no. 4 (2005): 289.

7. See T. Canli et al., "Sex Differences in the Neural Basis of Emotional Memories," *Proceedings of the National Academy of Science USA* 99 (2002): 10789–94; Larry Cahill et al., "Sex-Related Hemispherical Lateralization of Amygdala Function in Emotionally Influenced Memory: An fMRI Investigation," *Learning and Memory* 11 (2004): 261–66.

8. Also see chapters 4 ("Brain Plasticity and Homosexuality") and 6 ("Heterosexual and Homosexual Brain Differences") in my work *Born This Way? Homosexuality, Science, and the Scriptures* (Wooster, OH: Weaver, 2016), for more on brain differences.

9. As an example, compare conflicting data about the hippocampus. Larry Cahill, "His Brain, Her Brain," *Scientific American*, May 2005, 44. Contradicting Cahill is A. Tan et al., "The Human Hippocampus Is Not Sexually Dimorphic: Meta-analysis of Structural MRI Volumes," *Neuroimage* 124 (January 1, 2016): 350–66.

10. G. Rametti et al., "White Matter Microstructure in Female to Male Transsexuals before Cross-Sex Hormonal Treatment: A Diffusion Tensor Imaging Study," *Journal of Psychiatric Research* 45, no. 2 (2011): 199–204; E. Hoekzema et al., "Regional Volumes and Spatial Volumetric Distribution of Gray Matter in the Gender Dysphoric Brain," *Psychoneuroendocrinology* 55 (May 2015): 59–71.

11. Simon LeVay, "A Difference in Hypothalamic Structure between Heterosexual and Homosexual Men," *Science* 253 (August 30, 1991): 1034–37.

12. Alicia Garcia-Galgueras and Dick F. Swaab, "A Sex Difference in the Hypothalamic Uncinate Nucleus; Relationship to Gender Identity," *Brain* 131 (2008): 3132–46. In 2011, the same group claimed to find that the INAH 1 in MtF transsexuals had neuronal numbers between heterosexual men and heterosexual women. Alicia Garcia-Galgueras et al., "Galanin Neurons in the Intermediate Nucleus of the Human Hypothalamus in Relation to Sex, Age, and Gender Identity," *Journal of Comparative Neurology* 519 (October 15, 2011): 3061–84.

13. The authors say, "There was no difference in INAH 3 between pre- and post-menopausal women, either in volume or number of neurons, indicating that feminization of the INAH 3 of male-to-female transsexuals was not due to estrogen treatment." Garcia-Galgueras and Swaab, "Sex Difference," 3132.

14. Hilleke E. Hulshoff Pol et al., "Changing Your Sex Changes Your Brain: Influences of Testosterone and Estrogen on Adult Human Brain Structure," *European Journal of Endocrinology* 144 (November 1, 2006): 113.

15. L. Zubiaurre-Elorza et al., "Effects of Cross-Sex Hormone Treatment on Cortical Thickness In Transsexual Individuals," *Journal of Sexual Medicine* 11, no. 5 (2014): 1248–61.

16. Eric C. Dumont, "What Is the Bed Nucleus of the Stria Terminalis?," *Progress In Neuro-Psychopharmacology and Biological Psychiatry* 33, no. 8 (2009): 1289. The BNST is sometimes called the extended amygdala.

17. David L. Walker, Donna J. Toufexis, and Michael Davis, "Role of the Bed Nucleus of the Stria Terminalis versus the Amygdala in Fear, Stress, and Anxiety," *European Journal of Pharmacology* 463 (2003): 199–216.

18. M. A. Lebow and A. Chen, "Overshadowed by the Amygdala: The BNST Emerges as Key to Psychiatric Disorders," *Molecular Psychiatry* 21 (2016): 450, 451.

19. Jiang-Ning Zhou et al., "A Sex Difference in the Human Brain and Its Relation to Transsexuality," *Nature* 378 (November 1995): 68.

20. Zhou et al., "A Sex Difference," 70.

21. See Swaab's diagram at Zhou et al., "A Sex Difference," 70.

22. Zhou et al., "A Sex Difference," 70.

23. Frank P. M. Kruijver et al., "Male-to-Female Transsexuals Have Female Neuron Numbers in a Limbic Nucleus," *Journal of Clinical Endocrinology and Metabolism* 8, no. 5 (2000): 2036.

24. Wilson C. J. Chung, Geert J. De Vries, and Dick F. Swaab, "Sexual Differentiation of the Bed Nucleus of the Stria Terminalis in Humans May Extend Into Adulthood," *Journal of Neuroscience* 22, no. 3 (2002): 1027, 1031.

25. Chung, De Vries, and Swaab, "Sexual Differentiation," 1032.

26. Giuseppina Rametti et al., "White Matter Microstructure in Female to Male Transsexuals Before Cross-Sex Hormonal Treatment: A Diffusion Tensor Imaging Study," *Journal of Psychiatric Research* 45, no. 2 (2011): 199–204; Giuseppina Rametti et al., "The Microstructure of White Matter in Male to Female Transsexuals Before Cross-Sex Hormonal Treatment: A DTI Study," *Journal of Psychiatric Research* 45, no. 7 (2011): 949–54.

27. George S. Kranz et al., "Cerebral Serotonin Transporter Asymmetry in Females, Males and Male-To-Female Transsexuals Measured by PET in Vivo," *Brain Structure and Function* 219, no. 1 (2014): 171–83; George S. Kranz et al., "White Matter Microstructure in Transsexuals and Controls Investigated by Diffusion Tensor Imaging," *Journal of Neuroscience* 34, no. 46 (2014): 15466–75.

28. Elke Stefanie Smith et al., "The Transsexual Brain: A Review of Findings on the Neural Basis of Transsexualism," *Neuroscience and Biobehavioral Reviews* 59 (2015): 254. These authors emphasize that both studies indicate that transsexuals have a different white matter structure, which appears more like their desired sex.

29. Antonio Guillamon, Carme Junque, and Esther Gomez-Gil, "A Review of the Status of Brain Structure Research in Transsexualism," *Archives of Sexual Behavior* 45 (2016): 1643.

30. Milton Diamond, "Transsexuality among Twins: Identity Concordance, Transition, Rearing, and Orientation," *International Journal of Transgenderism* 14, no. 1 (2013): 34.

31. Lawrence Mayer and Paul McHugh, "Special Report: Sexuality and Gender," *The New Atlantis* 50 (fall 2016): 103.

32. Mayer and McHugh, "Special Report," 103.

33. Lucian R. Piccolo et al., "Age-Related Differences in Cortical Thickness Vary by Socioeconomic Status," *PLOS One* 11, no. 9 (2016): https://journals.plos.org/plosone/article?id=10.1371/journal.pone.0162511.

34. Stuart J. Ritchie et al., "Sex Differences in the Adult Human Brain: Evidence from 5,215 UK Biobank Participants," *BioRxiv*, April 4, 2017, http://www.biorxiv.org/content/early/2017/04/04/123729.article-info.

35. Diamond, "Transsexuality among Twins," 34.

36. Swaab and Garcia-Falgueras, "Sexual Differentiation," 24.

Chapter 6: Hormonal Treatment of Gender Dysphoria

1. Dave Quinn, "Jazz Jennings Gets Real about the 'Complications' Delaying Her Bottom Surgery: It's a "Very Serious Procedure," *People TV Watch*, June 20, 2017, http://people.com/tv/jazz-jennings-transgender-bottom-surgery-complications/.

2. Richard Green, "Gender Development and Reassignment," *Psychiatry* 6, no. 3 (2007): 123.

3. This list is derived from the World Professional Association for Transgender Health, *Standards of Care for the Health of Transsexual, Transgender, and Gender Nonconforming People*, 7th ed., 34, 59, 60, https://wpath.org/publications/soc.

4. Craig Kline and David Schrock, "What Is Gender Reassignment? A Medical Assessment with a Biblical Appraisal," *Journal for Biblical Manhood and Womanhood* 20, no. 1 (2015): 37.

5. Wylie C. Hembree et al., "Endocrine Treatment of Transsexual Persons: An Endocrine Society Clinical Practice Guideline," *Journal of Clinical Endocrinology and Metabolism* 94, no. 9 (2009): 3143.

6. If an MtF has his testes removed, the antiandrogen hormones are then stopped.

7. Marshall Dahl et al., "Physical Aspects of Transgender Endocrine Therapy," *International Journal of Transgenderism* 9, nos. 3-4 (2006): 115.

8. Serum testosterone levels are lower with transdermal administration via a patch or gel as opposed to an intramuscular injection. Louis J. Gooren, "Care of Transsexual Persons," *New England Journal of Medicine* 364, no. 13 (2011): 1253.

9. Hembree et al., "Endocrine Treatment of Transsexual Persons," 3145.

10. Louis J. Gooren, "Hormone Treatment of Adult Transgender People," in *Principles of Transgender Medicine and Surgery*, ed. Randi Ettner, Stan Monstrey, and Eli Coleman, 2nd ed. (New York: Routledge, 2016), 170.

11. Testicular volume is reduced by up to 25 percent in the first year, with gradual reduction of up to 50 percent of the original volume over a long period of time. Dahl et al., "Physical Aspects of Transgender Endocrine Therapy," 113.

12. Hembree et al., "Endocrine Treatment of Transsexual Persons," 3145.

13. Kevin Richard Wylie et al., "Recommendations of Endocrine Treatment for Patients with Gender Dysphoria," *Sexual and Relationship Therapy* 24, no. 2 (2009): 183.

14. Hair on the body grows more quickly while facial hair takes longer to develop.

15. In approximately 75 percent of FtMs, testosterone will cause voice pitch to drop to a level sufficient to pass as male even on the telephone. Dahl et al., "Physical Aspects of Transgender Endocrine Therapy," 118.

16. One study from Belgium indicated 5.1 percent of MtF experienced venous thrombosis and/or pulmonary embolism during hormone therapy. Almost half of these incidents occurred during the first year of treatment and another three at the time of the GRS. K. Wierckx et al., "Prevalence of Cardiovascular Disease

and Cancer During Cross-Sex Hormone Therapy in a Large Cohort of Trans Persons: A Case-Control Study," *European Journal of Endocrinology* 169 (2013): 475.

17. A 1997 study claimed to find no increased morbidity in either MtFs or FtMs. P. J. van Kesteren et al., "Mortality and Morbidity in Transsexual Subjects Treated with Cross-Sex Hormones," *Clinical Endocrinology* 47, no. 3 (1997): 337–42. These claims were hampered by methodological limitations. Dahl et al., "Physical Aspects of Transgender Endocrine Therapy," 119.

18. H. Asschemann et al., "A Long-Term Follow-Up Study of Mortality In Transsexuals Receiving Treatment with Cross-Sex Hormones," *European Journal of Endocrinology* 164, no. 4 (2011): 635–42.

19. Jamie D. Weinand and Joshua D. Safer, "Hormone Therapy in Transgender Adults Is Safe with Provider Supervision: A Review of Hormone Therapy Sequelae for Transgender Individuals," *Journal of Clinical and Translational Endocrinology* 2, no. 2 (2015): 55–60.

20. D. S. Dizon et al., "Ovarian Cancer Associated with Testosterone Supplementation in a Female-to-Male Transsexual Patient," *Gynecologic and Obstetric Investigation* 62, no. 4 (2006): 226–28.

21. Gooren, "Care of Transsexual Persons," 1254.

22. Dahl et al., "Physical Aspects of Transgender Endocrine Therapy," 118.

23. Dahl et al., "Physical Aspects of Transgender Endocrine Therapy," 113, 114.

24. P. T. Cohen-Kettenis and S. H. van Goozen, "Pubertal Delay as an Aid in Diagnosis and Treatment of a Transsexual Adolescent," *European Child and Adolescent Psychiatry* 7, no. 4 (1998): 246–48.

25. This summary from Jason Lambrese, "Journal Discussion: Suppression of Puberty in Transgender Children," *American Medical Association Journal of Ethics* 12, no. 8 (2010): 646. GnRH drugs are expensive, and progestins can be used as an alternative treatment. Furthermore, antiestrogens in girls and antiandrogens in boys delay the progression of puberty, although neither is as effective as GnRH. Louis J. Gooren, "Care of Transsexual Persons," *New England Journal of Medicine* 364, no. 13 (2011): 1255.

26. For example, see the Human Rights Campaign, "Supporting and Caring for Transgender Children," September 2016, http://www.hrc.org/resources/supporting-caring-for-transgender-children.

27. Henriette A. Delemarre-van de Waal and Peggy T. Cohen-Kettenis, "Clinical Management of Gender Identity Disorder in Adolescents: A Protocol on Psychological and Paediatric Endocrinology," *European Journal of Endocrinology* 155 (2006): S136–S137.

28. Delemarre-van de Waal and Peggy T. Cohen-Kettenis, "Clinical Management," S137.

29. Delemarre-van de Waal and Peggy T. Cohen-Kettenis, "Clinical Management," S137. They stressed that preliminary data indicates no long-term problems with the brain.

30. Annemeike S. Staphorsius et al., "Puberty Suppression and Executive Functioning: An fMRI-Study in Adolescents with Gender Dysphoria," *Psychoneuroendocrinology* 56 (June 2015): 197.

31. Paul W. Hruz, Lawrence S. Mayer, and Paul R. McHugh, "Growing Pains: Problems with Puberty Suppression in Treating Gender Dysphoria," *The New Atlantis* 52 (spring 2017): 24.

32. *Diagnostic and Statistical Manual of Mental Disorders V* (Arlington, VA: American Psychiatric Association, 2013), 454.

33. Peggy T. Cohen-Kettenis, Henriette A. Delemarre-van de Waal, and Louis J. G. Gooren, "The Treatment of Adolescent Transsexuals: Changing Insights," *Journal of Sexual Medicine* 5 (2008): 1895. The authors state that none of the children treated at the Gender Identity Clinic at the Free University dropped out of the program and all continued to sex reassignment.

34. Hruz, Mayer, and McHugh, "Growing Pains," 19–20.

35. Cohen-Kettenis et al., "Treatment of Adolescent Transsexuals," 1894.

36. See Mariam Araiin et al., "Maturation of the Adolescent Brain," *Neuropsychiatric Disease and Treatment* 9 (2013): 449–61.

Chapter 7: Gender Reassignment Surgery

1. Renée Richards with John Ames, *Second Serve* (New York: Stein and Day, 1984), 282, 281.

2. The World Professional Association for Transgender Health, *Standards of Care for the Health of Transsexual, Transgender, and Gender Nonconforming People*, 7th ed., 2010, 54–55, https://www.wpath.org/publications/soc.

3. P. J. van Kestern, L. J. Gooren, and J. A. Megens, "An Epidemiological and Demographic Study of Transsexuals in The Netherlands," *Archives of Sexual Behavior* 25, no. 6 (1996): 589–600.

4. For example, see D. Duisin, G. Nikolić-Balkoski, and B. Batinić, "Sociodemographic Profile of Transsexual Patients," *Psychiatria Danubina* 21, no. 2 (2009): 220–23, which reported that in Serbia males asked for GRS more than females at a rate of 3:2. In Iran, there is some evidence of more FtM surgeries, but data is not certain. See A. Hedjazi et al., "Socio-demographic Characteristics of Transsexuals Referred to the Forensic Medicine Center in Southwest Iran," *North American Journal of Medical Sciences* 5, no. 3 (2013): 224–27.

5. B. Reed et al., "Gender Variance in the UK: Prevalence, Incidence, Growth, and Geographic Distribution," Gender Identity Research and Education Society, June 2009, https://www.gires.org.uk/wp-content/uploads/2014/10/GenderVarianceUK-report.pdf. There is apparently some variation among certain ethnic groups, with a 2011 report claiming a higher rate of FtM than MtF transsexualism in Japan. Tsuyoshi Baba et al., "Distinctive Features of Female-to-Male Transsexualism and Prevalence of Gender Identity Disorder in Japan," *Journal of Sexual Medicine* 8, no. 6 (2011): 1686–93.

6. American Society of Plastic Surgeons, "First Ever Data on Number of Gender Confirmation Surgeries," May 22, 2017, https://www.plasticsurgery.org/news/press-releases/gender-confirmation-surgeries-rise-20-percent-in-first-ever-report.

7. "U.S. Gender Confirmation Surgery Up 19% in 2016, Doctors Say," *NBC News*, May 22, 2019, http://www.nbcnews.com/feature/nbc-out/u-s-gender-confirmation-surgery-19-2016-doctors-say-n762916. The story was originally released by Reuters, but Reuters withdrew the story because of questions surrounding the ASPS data.

8. For example, on May 30, 2014, the Obama Administration's Department of Health and Human Services Departmental Appeals Board reversed a long-standing rule that GRS would not be covered by Medicare. Department

of Health and Human Services, "Access to Health Care: Non-Discrimination-Transgender," August 15, 2017, https://www.hhs.gov/programs/topic-sites/lgbt/accesstohealthcare/nondiscrimination/index.html. In 2016, the Centers for Medicare and Medicaid Services issued a memo that declined to make a National Coverage Determination regarding GRS, but instead suggested continuing the practice of evaluating each request on a case-by-case basis. See Tamara Syrek Jensen et al., "Proposed Decision Memo for Gender Dysphoria and Gender Reassignment Surgery," Centers for Medicare and Medicaid Services, June 2, 2016, https://www.cms.gov/medicare-coverage-database/details/nca-proposed-decision-memo.aspx?NCAId=282.

9. Gennaro Selvaggi and James Bellringer, "Gender Reassignment Surgery: An Overview," *Nature Review of Urology* 8, no. 5 (2011): 274.

10. Britt Colebunders et al., "Male-to-Female Gender Reassignment," *Principles of Transgender Medicine and Surgery*, ed. Randi Ettner, Stan Monstrey, and Eli Coleman, 2nd ed. (New York: Routledge, 2016), 259. Others suggest MtF "top surgery" should be considered only if breasts have not reached a desired size after 18–24 months of hormone use. Marshall Dahl et al., "Physical Aspects of Transgender Endocrine Therapy," *International Journal of Transgenderism* 9, nos. 3–4 (2006): 113.

11. Colebunders et al., "Male-to-Female Gender Reassignment," 260.

12. Selvaggi and Bellringer, "Gender Reassignment," 278.

13. Colebunders et al., "Male-to-Female Gender Reassignment," 264.

14. Selvaggi and Bellringer, "Gender Reassignment Surgery," 276.

15. Burin Wangjiraniran et al., "Male-to-Female Vaginoplasty: Preecha's Surgical Technique," *Journal of Plastic Surgery and Hand Surgery* 49, no. 3 (2015): 156–57, 158. See also, P. A. Sutcliffe et al., "Evaluation of Surgical Procedures for Sex Reassignment: A Systematic Review," *Journal of Plastic, Reconstructive and Aesthetic Surgery* 62, no. 3 (2009): 299.

16. Peggy T. Cohen-Kettenis and Thomas D. Steensma, "Gender Dysphoria," in *APA Handbook of Clinical Psychology*, vol. 4, *Psychopathology and Health*, ed. John C. Norcross et al. (Washington, DC: American Psychological Association, 2016), 401.

17. Colebunders et al., "Male-to-Female Gender Reassignment Surgery," 269.

18. Selvaggi and Bellringer, "Gender Reassignment Surgery," 276.

19. Craig Kline and David Schrock, "What Is Gender Reassignment? A Medical Assessment with a Biblical Appraisal," *Journal for Biblical Manhood and Womanhood* 20, no. 1 (2015): 40.

20. M. H. Sohn, M. Hatzinger, and K. Wirsam, "Genital Reassignment Surgery in Male-to-Female Transsexuals: Do We Have Guidelines or Standards?," *Handchirurgie Mikrochirurgie Plastiche Chirurgie* 45, no. 4 (2013): 207–10.

21. Selvaggi and Bellringer, "Gender Reassignment Surgery," 277.

22. Colebunders et al., "Male-to-Female Gender Reassignment Surgery," 272.

23. Removal of breasts, ovaries, and uterus is often recommended for FtM because cancer is not easily detected in these organs. Louis J. Gooren, "Care of Transsexual Persons," *New England Journal of Medicine* 364, no. 13 (2011): 1255.

24. Sutcliffe et al., "Evaluation of Surgical Procedures," 299.

25. For example, see Britt Colebunders et al., "Female-to-Male Gender Reassignment Surgery," in Ettner, Monstrey, and Coleman, *Principles of Transgender Medicine and Surgery*, 293.

26. Selvaggi and Bellringer, "Gender Reassignment Surgery," 280.

27. Colebunders et al., "Female-to-Male Gender Reassignment Surgery," 296. In such cases, the urethral opening is left at the base of the imitation penis.

28. Colebunders et al., "Female-to-Male Gender Reassignment Surgery," 297.

29. Sutcliffe et al., "Evaluation of Surgical Procedures," 301.

30. Harry Benjamin, *The Transsexual Phenomenon* (New York: Julian, 1966), 113.

31. Benjamin, *Transsexual Phenomenon*, 46.

32. Gooren, "Hormone Treatment of Adult Transgender People," 168. Gooren favors GRS.

33. It is with some frustration that one reads Louis Gooren say, "Transsexuals may not always be forthright with physicians about their sex change, and this hesitancy can lead to delays in *diagnosing cancers of organs specific to the former sex*." Gooren, "Care of Transsexual Persons," 1254 (emphasis added). But the reason such people have these organs—for example, a prostate in an MtF—is because what Gooren calls their "former sex" is their actual sex!

34. Kline and Schrock, "What Is Gender Reassignment Surgery?," 37.

35. Richard Fitzgibbons, Philip M. Sutton, and Dale O'Leary, "The Psychopathology of 'Sex Reassignment' Surgery: Assessing Its Medical, Psychological, and Ethical Appropriateness," *National Catholic Bioethics Center* (2009): 98.

36. Richards, *Second Serve*, 281.

37. See Chantal M. Wiepjes et al., "The Amsterdam Cohort of Gender Dysphoria Study (1972–2015): Trends in Prevalence, Treatment, and Regrets," *Journal of Sexual Medicine* 15, no. 4 (2018): 582–90.

38. A 2014 study from Sweden claimed 2.2 percent regret GRS, but the criteria used to define the sample has limitations. Cecilia Dhejne et al., "An Analysis of All Applications for Sex Reassignment Surgery in Sweden, 1960–2010: Prevalence, Incidence, and Regrets," *Archives of Sexual Behavior* 43, no. 8 (2014): 1535–45.

39. M. L. Jordjevic et al., "Reversal Surgery in Regretful Male-to-Female Transsexuals after Sex Reassignment Surgery," *Journal of Sexual Medicine* 13, no. 6 (2016): 1000–1007.

40. M. H. Murad et al., "Hormonal Therapy and Sex Reassignment: A Systematic Review and Meta-analysis of Quality of Life and Psychosocial Outcomes," *Clinical Endocrinology* 72, no. 2 (2010): 214–31.

41. Nonetheless, Richard Raskind reflects the attitude of many people who have "transitioned" and said that in spite of the pain "not once did I wish I hadn't done it. There was no remorse in spite of the suffering." Richards, *Second Serve*, 281.

42. S. Krege et al., "Male-to-Female Transsexualism: A Technique, Results, and Long-Term Follow Up in 66 Patients," *British Journal of Urology* 88 (2001): 396–402.

43. Sutcliffe et al., "Evaluation of Surgical Procedures," 302.

44. Sutcliffe et al., "Evaluation of Surgical Procedures," 302.

45. Cecilia Dhejne et al., "Long-Term Follow-Up of Transsexual Persons Undergoing Sex-Reassignment Surgery: Cohort Study in Sweden," *PloS One* 6, no. 2 (2011): 7.

46. Dhejne et al., "Long-Term Follow-Up," 7.

47. J. Schaff and N. A. Papadopulos, "A New Protocol for Complete Phalloplasty With Free Sensate and Prelaminated Osteofasciocutaneous Flaps: Experience in 37 Patients," *Microsurgery* 29, no. 5 (2009): 413–19.

48. Colebunders et al., "Female-to-Male Gender Reassignment Surgery," 296.

49. Mamoon Rashid and Muhammad Sarmad Tamimy, "Phalloplasty: The Dream and the Reality," *Indian Journal of Plastic Surgery* 46, no. 2 (2013): 283–93.

50. Rashid and Tamimy, "Phalloplasty," 298.

51. Samuel Golpanian et al., "Phalloplasty and Urethral (Re)construction: A Chronological Timeline," *Anaplastology* 5, no. 2 (2016): 5.

52. Green, "Gender Development and Reassignment," 123.

53. Selvaggi and Bellringer, "Gender Reassignment Surgery," 277.

54. Selvaggi and Bellringer, "Gender Reassignment Surgery," 277.

55. Green, "Gender Development and Reassignment," 123.

56. World Professional Association for Transgender Health, *Standards of Care*.

57. People with this disorder experience a difference between their internal body scheme and physical body shape. Rianne M. Blom et al., "The Desire for Amputation or Paralyzation: Evidence for Structural Brain Anomalies in Body Integrity Identity Disorder," *PloS One* 11, no. 11 (2016): 2, http://journals.plos.org/plosone/article?id=10.1371/journal.pone.0165789.

58. Oliver O'Donovan, *Transsexualism and Christian Marriage* (Bramcote, UK: Grove, 1982), 16.

59. My thoughts here are influenced by Kline and Schrock, "What Is Gender Reassignment Surgery?," 43.

60. Cohen-Kettenis and Steensma, "Gender Dysphoria," 398.

61. C. E. B. Cranfield, *Romans IX–XVI*, International Critical Commentary (Edinburgh: T&T Clark, 1979), 609.

62. I recognize that in context Paul is addressing false beliefs in the Corinthian church, but Murray Harris acknowledges this and adds, "But we should also recognize a general reference to faulty patterns of thought that Paul knew from personal experience to be characteristic of unbelievers and that hindered their response to the Gospel of Christ." Murray J. Harris, *The Second Epistle to the Corinthians*, New International Greek Testament Commentary (Grand Rapids: Eerdmans, 2005), 683.

63. Jonathan Edwards, *The Works of Jonathan Edwards*, vol. 2, *A Treatise Concerning Religious Affections*, ed. John E. Smith (New Haven CT: Yale University Press, 1959), 434.

64. Edwards, *Religious Affections*, 429.

Chapter 8: Transgenderism and the Family

1. Michele Angello and Alisa Bowman, *Raising the Transgender Child: A Complete Guide for Parents, Families, and Caregivers* (Berkeley, CA: Seal Press, 2016), 173.

2. Nicholas M. Teich, "Why Jenner's Interview Makes the Case for Supporting Transgender Youth Now," *Huffington Post*, April 28, 2015, http://www

.huffingtonpost.com/nicholas-m-teich/why-jenners-interview-mak_b_7157038
.html.

3. GLSEN and the National Center for Transgender Identity, "Model District Policy on Transgender and Gender Nonconforming Students," February 2016, 8, https://www.glsen.org/sites/default/files/Trans%20Model%20Policy.pdf.

4. Mary Emily O'Hara, "Minnesota Mom Sues Her Trans Child Over Gender Reassignment," *NBC News*, November 17, 2016, https://www.nbcnews.com/feature/nbc-out/minnesota-mom-sues-her-trans-child-over-gender-reassignment-n685266. The case is complicated by the parents' divorce.

5. O'Hara, "Minnesota Mom."

6. *Diagnostic and Statistical Manual of Mental Disorders V* (Arlington, VA: American Psychiatric Association, 2013), 454.

7. *DSM V*, 455. From my perspective, reasons for the broad ranges include difficulties in getting a good sample and variations in the ways "transgender" or "gender non-conformity" are defined.

8. Mark Yarhouse, *Understanding Gender Dysphoria: Navigating Transgender Issues in a Changing Culture* (Downers Grove, IL: IVP Academic, 2015), 101.

9. Thomas D. Steensma et al., "Desisting and Persisting Gender Dysphoria after Childhood: A Qualitative Follow-Up Study," *Clinical Child Psychology and Psychiatry* 16, no. 4 (2011): 499–516.

10. Madeleine S. C. Wallien and Peggy T. Cohen-Kettenis, "Psychosexual Outcome of Gender-Dysphoric Children," *Journal of the American Academy of Child and Adolescent Psychiatry* 47, no. 12 (2008): 1413

11. Yarhouse, *Understanding Gender Dysphoria*, 103.

12. Angello and Bowman, *Raising the Transgender Child*, 19.

13. *DSM V*, 455.

14. Wallien and Cohen-Kettenis, "Psychosexual Outcome," 1421.

15. Steensma et al., "Desisting and Persisting," 13.

16. Johanna Olson et al., "Baseline Physiologic and Psychosocial Characteristics of Transgender Youth Seeking Care for Gender Dysphoria," *Journal of Adolescent Health* 57, no. 4 (2015): 374–80.

17. Yarhouse, *Understanding Gender Dysphoria*, 106.

18. Stanton L. Jones and Brenna B. Jones, *How and When to Tell Your Kids about Sex* (Colorado Springs, CO: NavPress, 1993), 81.

19. Diane Ehrensaft, "Boys Will Be Girls, Girls Will Be Boys," *Psychoanalytic Psychology* 28, no. 4 (2011): 542.

20. Nicholas M. Teich, *Transgender 101: A Simple Guide to a Complex Issue* (New York: Columbia University Press, 2012), 32.

21. Ann McNary, "Consent to Treatment of Minors," *Innovations in Clinical Neuroscience* 11, nos. 3–4 (2014): 43.

22. Emily Ikuta said, "Adolescents who suffer from gender dysphoria should have the option of taking hormone blockers that delay puberty ... *even in the absence of parental consent.*" Emily Ikuta, "Overcoming Parental Veto: How Transgender Adolescents Can Access Puberty-Suppressing Hormone Treatment in the Absence of Parental Consent Under the Mature Minor Doctrine," *Southern California Interdisciplinary Law Journal* 25 (2016): 182.

23. Ann P. Haas et al., "Suicide and Suicide Risk in Lesbian, Gay, Bisexual, and Transgender Populations: Review and Recommendations," *Journal of Homosexuality* 58 (2011): 27.

24. These excerpts from Alcorn's note found in Steve Helling and Myndi Milliken, "Transgender Teen Leelah Alcorn Driven to Suicide?," *People*, January 19, 2015, 50.

25. Many critics of the family acted as if taking away cellphone and social media privileges were denying the child basic human rights.

26. Harold W. Hoehner, *Ephesians: An Exegetical Commentary* (Grand Rapids: Baker Academic, 2002), 796.

27. Joel Frader et al., "Health Care Professionals and Intersex Conditions," *Archives of Pediatrics and Adolescent Medicine* 158 (2004): 426.

28. Cara Megan Ogilvie et al., "Congenital Adrenal Hyperplasia in Adults: A Review of Medical, Surgical and Psychological Issues," *Clinical Endocrinology* 64 (2006): 2–11.

29. I. A. Hughes et al., "Consensus Statement On Management of Intersex Disorders," *Archives of Disease in Childhood* 91, no. 7 (2006): 556–57.

30. While genetic tests should be the primary method of determining the correct gender, we must also acknowledge cases such as androgen insensitivity syndrome, in which children are born "XY," but their bodies develop as females, except they lack a uterus and ovaries.

Chapter 9: Transgenderism, Christian Living, and the Ministry of the Local Church

1. Devin Friedman, "Kristen Beck: A Navy Seal in Transition," *GQ*, November 25, 2015, https://www.gq.com/story/kristin-beck-transgender-navy-seal.

2. Kristen Beck, "Transgender Ex-Navy Seal: Here's a Question for You," CNN, September 2, 2014, http://www.cnn.com/2014/09/02/opinion/lady-valor-kristin-beck-transgender-navy-seal/index.html.

3. Annamarie Jagose and Don Kulick, "Thinking Sex / Thinking Gender," *GLQ: A Journal of Gay and Lesbian Studies* 10, no. 2 (2004): 211. Jagose is a professor at the University of Sydney and Kulick is a professor of anthropology at Uppsala University.

4. For example, the appendixes to Harry Benjamin's *The Transsexual Phenomenon* include the story of a man who was raped and sodomized at age fifteen. The comment is added, "This resulted in a severe sphincter laceration and probably psychological trauma." Harry Benjamin, *The Transsexual Phenomenon* (New York: Julian, 1966), 264.

5. Anette Kersting et al., "Dissociative Disorders and Traumatic Childhood Experiences in Transsexuals," *Journal of Nervous and Mental Disease* 19, no. 1 (2003): 182–89.

6. Nicholas Teich, *Transgender 101: A Simple Guide to a Complex Issue* (New York: Columbia University Press, 2012), 94.

7. Michele Angello and Alisa Bowman, *Raising the Transgender Child: A Complete Guide for Parents, Families, and Caregivers* (Berkeley, CA: Seal Press, 2016), 125.

8. My words here influenced by Darrell L. Bock, *Luke 9:51–24:53*, Baker Exegetical Commentary on the New Testament (Grand Rapids: Baker Academic, 1996), 1144.

9. See chapter 2, subsection titled "Transvestites."

10. For example, writing in 1969, Richard Green said, "The transvestite is typically heterosexual, and considers himself a male when dressed as a man, though to varying degrees he may consider himself to be a woman when dressed as one. Cross-dressing may be sexually exciting, thus taking on fetishistic qualities." Richard Green, "Psychiatric Management of Special Problems in Transsexualism," in *Transsexualism and Sex Reassignment*, ed. Richard Green and John Money (Baltimore: Johns Hopkins University Press, 1969), 282.

11. Renée Richards with John Ames, *Second Serve* (New York: Stein and Day, 1983), 207.

12. Harold W. Hoehner, *Ephesians: An Exegetical Commentary* (Grand Rapids: Baker Academic, 2002), 824.

13. Richards with Ames, *Second Serve*, 84.

14. Rita M. Melendez and Rogerio Pinto, "'It's a Really Hard Life': Love, Gender and HIV Risk among Male to Female Transgender Persons," *Culture, Health, and Sexuality* 9, no. 3 (2007): 233–45, https://www.ncbi.nlm.nih.gov/pmc/articles/PMC3539165/?report=reader.

15. One source emphasizes that after GRS, continued administration of cross-sex hormones is required to avoid symptoms and signs of hormone deficiency, such as vasomotor symptoms and, in particular, osteoporosis. Louis J. Gooren, "Care of Transsexual Persons," *New England Journal of Medicine* 364, no. 13 (2011): 1253.

16. "On Transgender Identity," A Resolution Adopted by the Southern Baptist Convention Meeting in Baltimore, MD, June 10–11, 2014, http://www.sbc.net/resolutions/2250/on-transgender-identity.

17. Augustine, *The City of God against the Pagans*, trans. Philp Levine, Loeb Classical Library 4 (Cambridge, MA: Harvard University Press, 1966), 275, 14.4.

SELECT BIBLIOGRAPHY

GENERAL RESOURCES

American Psychological Association. "Answers to Your Questions about Transgender People, Gender Identity and Gender Expression." 2014. http://www.apa.org/topics/lgbt/transgender.pdf.

Beatie, Thomas. *Labor of Love: The Story of One Man's Extraordinary Pregnancy.* Berkeley, CA: Seal Press, 2008.

Benjamin, Harry. *The Transsexual Phenomenon.* New York: Julian, 1966.

Beauvoir, Simone de. *The Second Sex.* Translated by Constance Borde and Sheila Malovany-Chevallier. New York: Vintage, 2011.

Bradley, Susan J., and Kenneth J. Zucker. "Gender Identity Disorder: A Review of the Past 10 Years." *Journal of the American Academy of Child and Adolescent Psychiatry* 36, no. 9 (1997): 872–80.

Bullough, Vern L. "Magnus Hirschfeld: An Often Overlooked Pioneer." *Sexuality and Culture* 7, no. 1 (2003): 62–73.

———. *Science in the Bedroom.* New York: Basic Books, 1994.

Burnes, Theodore R. Anneliese A. Singh, Amney Harper, Denise L. Pickering, Sean Moundas, Thomas Scofield, Will Maxon, Brandon Harper, Alex Roan, and Julia Hosea. "Competencies for Counseling Transgender Clients." Association for Lesbian, Gay, Bisexual, and

Transgender Issues in Counseling. November 7, 2009. https://www.counseling.org/Resources/Competencies/ALGBTIC_Competencies.pdf.

Cauldwell, David O. "Psychopathia Transsexualis." *Sexology* 16 (December 1949): 274–80.

Cohen-Kettenis, Peggy T., and Thomas D. Steensma. "Gender Dysphoria." In *APA Handbook of Clinical Psychology*. Vol. 4, *Psychopathology and Health*, edited by John C. Norcross, Gary R. VandenBos, Donald K. Freedheim, and Nnamdi Pole, 395–406. Washington, DC: American Psychological Association, 2016.

Colapinto, John. *As Nature Made Him: The Boy Who Was Raised as a Girl.* New York: HarperCollins, 2001.

Colin, Lindsay, Michael Goodman, and Vin Tangpricha. "Worldwide Prevalence of Transgender and Gender Non-conformity." In *Principles of Transgender Medicine and Surgery*, edited by Randi Ettner, Stan Monstrey, and Eli Coleman, 16–35. 2nd ed. New York: Routledge, 2016.

Diagnostic and Statistical Manual of Mental Disorders. Washington, DC: American Psychiatric Association Mental Hospital Service, 1952.

Diagnostic and Statistical Manual of Mental Disorders II. Washington, DC: American Psychiatric Association, 1968.

Diagnostic and Statistical Manual of Mental Disorders III. Washington, DC: American Psychiatric Association, 1980.

Diagnostic and Statistical Manual of Mental Disorders IV–TR. Washington, DC: American Psychiatric Association, 2000.

Diagnostic and Statistical Manual of Mental Disorders V. Arlington, VA: American Psychiatric Association, 2013.

Diamond, Milton, and H. Keith Sigmundson. "Sex-Reassignment at Birth: Long-Term Review and Clinical

Implications." *Archives of Pediatrics and Adolescent Medicine* 151, no. 3 (1997): 298–304.

Erickson-Schroth, Laura, ed. *Trans Bodies Trans Selves: A Resource for the Transgender Community.* Oxford: Oxford University Press, 2014.

Fausto-Sterling, Anne. *Sexing the Body: Gender Politics and the Construction of Sexuality.* New York: Basic Books, 2000.

Flores, Andrew R., Jody L. Herman, Gary J. Yates, and Taylor N. T. Brown. "How Many Adults Identify as Transgender in the United States?" The Williams Institute. June 2016. https://williamsinstitute.law.ucla.edu/wp-content/uploads/How-Many-Adults-Identify-as-Transgender-in-the-United-States.pdf.

Frank, Walter. *Law and the Gay Rights Story.* New Brunswick, NJ: Rutgers University Press, 2014.

Gherovici, Patricia. *Please Select Your Gender.* New York: Routledge, 2010.

Gooren, Louis J. "Care of Transsexual Persons." *New England Journal of Medicine* 364, no. 13 (2011): 1251–57.

———. "Body Politics: The Physical Side of Gender Identity." In *John Money: A Tribute*, edited by Eli Coleman, 9–17. New York: Haworth, 1991.

Green, R., and E. B. Keverne. "The Disparate Maternal Aunt-Uncle Ratio in Male Transsexuals: An Explanation Invoking Genomic Imprinting." *Journal of Theoretical Biology* 202 (January 7, 2000): 55–63.

Haas, Ann P. "Suicide and Suicide Risk in Lesbian, Gay, Bisexual, and Transgender Populations: Review and Recommendations." *Journal of Homosexuality* 58 (2011): 10–51.

Herman, Jody, Andrew R. Flores, Taylor N.T. Brown, Bianca D.M. Wilson, and Kerith J. Conron. "Age of Individuals

Who Identify as Transgender in the United States."
The Williams Institute. January 2017. http://
williamsinstitute.law.ucla.edu/wp-content/uploads/
TransAgeReport.pdf.

Human Rights Campaign. "Resources on Gender-Expansive
Children and Youth?" http://www.hrc.org/resources/
resources-on-gender-expansive-children-and-youth.

Jagose, Annamarie, and Don Kulick. "Thinking Sex/Thinking
Gender." *GLQ: A Journal of Gay and Lesbian Studies* 10, no.
2 (2004): 211–12.

Kesteren, P. J., van, L. J. Gooren, J. A. Megens. "An
Epidemiological and Demographic Study of
Transsexuals in the Netherlands." *Archives of Sexual
Behavior* 25, no. 6 (1996): 589–600.

Kraemer, B., T. Noll, A. Delsignore, G. Milos, U. Schnyder, and
U. Hepp. "Finger Length Ratio (2D:4D) in Adults with
Gender Identity Disorder." *Archives of Sexual Behavior*
38, no. 3 (2009): 359–63.

Landé, M., J. Walinder, and B. Lundström. "Incidence and Sex
Ratio of Transsexualism in Sweden." *Acta Psychiatrica
Scandinavica* 93, no. 4 (1996): 261–63.

Levoy, Greg. "Transsexuals: Born in the Wrong Body."
Cincinnati Magazine, November 1984, 146–49.

Magnus Hirschfeld Society. "Institute for Sexual Science
(1919–1933)." http://magnus-hirschfeld.de/institute
-for-sexual-science-1919-1933/personnel/institute
-employees-and-domestic-personnel/.

Mayer, Lawrence S., and Paul R. McHugh. "Sexuality and
Gender: Findings from Biological, Psychological, and
Social Sciences." *The New Atlantis* 50 (fall 2016): 10–143.

McNary, Ann. "Consent to Treatment of Minors." *Innovations
in Clinical Neuroscience* 11 nos. 3–4 (2014): 43–45.

Meyerowitz, Joanne. *How Sex Changed: A History of Transsexuality in the United States*. Cambridge, MA: Harvard University Press, 2002.

Miller, Timothy. *The Hippies and American Values*. Knoxville: University of Tennessee Press, 1991.

Money, John, and Anke A. Ehrhardt. *Man and Woman, Boy and Girl*. Baltimore: Johns Hopkins University Press, 1972.

Nahas, Aili, Elizabeth Leonard, Jennifer Garcia, Raha Lewis, and Emily Strohm. "Bruce Jenner Opens Up about His Transition: Inside His Life Today." *People*. May 11, 2015, 44–50.

Savin-Williams, Ritch C. "The New Sexual Minority Teenager: Freedom from Traditional Notions of Sexual Identity." In *The Meaning of Sexual Identity in the Twenty-First Century*, edited by Judith S. Kaufman and David A. Powell, 4–20. Newcastle upon Tyne: Cambridge Scholars Publishing, 2014.

Schneider, H. J., J. Pickel, and G. K. Stalla. "Typical Female 2nd–4th Finger Length (2D:4D) Ratios in Male to Female Transsexuals: Possible Implications for Prenatal Androgen Exposure." *Psychoendocrinology* 31, no. 2 (2006): 265–69.

Sigusch, Volkmar. "The Neosexual Revolution." *Archives of Sexual Behavior* 27, no. 4 (1998): 331–59.

Stoller, Robert. *Sex and Gender: The Development of Masculinity and Femininity*. London: Karnac, 1968.

Tauber, Michelle, Jennifer Garcia, Pernilla Cedenheim, Steve Helling, Elizabeth Leonard, Raha Lewis, and Aili Nahas. "I Am Free: Bruce Jenner Is Now Caitlyn Jenner." *People*. June 15, 2015, 42–46

Teich, Nicolas M. *Transgender 101: A Simple Guide to a Complex Issue*. New York: Columbia University Press, 2012

Testa, Rylan Jay, Deborah Coolhart, and Jayme Peta. *The Gender Quest Workbook.* Oakland: Instant Help Books, 2015.

Wallien, Madeleine S. C., and Peggy T. Cohen-Kettenis. "Psychosexual Outcome of Gender-Dysphoric Children." *Journal of the American Academy of Child and Adolescent Psychiatry* 47, no. 12 (2008): 1413–23.

Wallien, Madeleine S., Kenneth J. Zucker, T. D. Steenmsma, and P. T. Cohen-Kettenis. "2D:4D Finger-Length Ratios in Children and Adults with Gender Identity Disorder." *Hormones and Behavior* 54, no. 3 (2008): 450–54.

Wylie, Kevan, et al. "Good Practice Guidelines for the Assessment and Treatment of Adults with Gender Dysphoria." *Sexual Relationship Therapy* 29, no. 2 (2014): 154–214.

Yarhouse, Mark A. *Understanding Gender Dysphoria.* Downers Grove, IL: IVP Academic, 2015.

Zucker, Kenneth J., R. Green C. Garofano, Susan J. Bradley, K. Williams, H. M. Rebach, and C. B. Sullivan. "Prenatal Gender Preference of Mothers of Feminine and Masculine Boys: Relation to Sibling Sex Composition and Birth Order." *Journal of Abnormal Child Psychology* 22, no. 1 (1994): 1–13.

Zucker, Kenneth J., Susan J. Bradley, and Moshe Ipp. "Delayed Naming of a Newborn Boy: Relationship to the Mother's Wish for a Girl and Subsequent Cross-Gender Identity in the Child by the Age of Two." *Journal of Psychology and Human Sexuality* 6, no. 1 (1994): 57–68.

BRAIN RESEARCH

Blom, Rianne M., Guido A. van Wingen, Sija J. van der Wal, Judy Luigjes, Milenna T. van Dijk, H. Steven Scholte, and Damiaan Denys. "The Desire for Amputation or

Paralyzation: Evidence for Structural Brain Anomalies in Body Integrity Identity Disorder." *PloS One* 11, no. 11 (2016): 1–13.

Chung, Wilson C. J., Geert J. De Vries, and Dick F. Swaab. "Sexual Differentiation of the Bed Nucleus of the Stria Terminalis in Humans May Extend into Adulthood." *Journal of Neuroscience* 22, no. 3 (2002): 1027–33.

Dörner, G., I. Poppe, F. Stahl, J. Kölzsch, and R. Uebelhack. "Gene-and Environment-Dependent Neuroendocrine Etiogenesis of Homosexuality and Transsexualism." *Experimental and Clinical Endocrinology* 98, no. 2 (1991): 141–50.

Dumont, Eric C. "What Is the Bed Nucleus of the Stria Terminalis?" *Progress in Neuro-Psychopharmacology and Biological Psychiatry* 33, no. 8 (2009): 1289–90.

Erickson-Schroth, Laura. "Update on the Biology of Transgender Identity." *Journal of Gay and Lesbian Mental Health* 17, no. 2 (2013): 150–74.

Garcia-Falqueras, A., and Dick Swaab. "Sexual Hormones and the Brain: An Essential Alliance for Sexual Identity and Sexual Orientation." *Endocrine Development* 17 (2010): 22–35.

Guillamon, Antonio, Carme Junque, and Esther Gómez-Gil. "A Review of the Status of Brain Structure Research in Transsexualism." *Archives of Sexual Behavior* 45 (2016): 1615–48.

Kranz, George S., Andreas Hahn, Pia Baldinger, Daniela Haeusler, Cecile Philippe, Ulrike Kaufmann, Wolfgang Wadsak, Markus Savli, Anna Hoeflich, Christoph Kraus, Thomas Vanicek, Markus Mitterhauser, Siegfried Kasper, Rupert Lanzenberger. "Cerebral Serotonin Transporter Asymmetry in Females, Males and Male-to-Female Transsexuals Measured by PET In Vivo." *Brain Structure and Function* 219, no. 1 (2014): 171–83.

Kranz, George S., Andreas Hahn, Ulrike Kaufmann, Martin Küblböck, Allan Hummer, Sebastian Ganger, Rene Seiger, Dietmar Winkler, Dick F. Swaab, Christian Windischberger, Siegfried Kasper, and Rupert Lanzenberger. "White Matter Microstructure in Transsexuals and Controls Investigated by Diffusion Tensor Imaging." *Journal of Neuroscience* 34, no. 46 (2014): 15466–75.

Kruijver, Frank P. M., Jiang-Ning Zhou, Chris W. Pool, Michel A. Hofman, Louis J. G. Gooren, and Dick Swaab. "Male-to-Female Transsexuals Have Female Neuron Numbers in a Limbic Nucleus." *Journal of Clinical Endocrinology and Metabolism* 85, no. 5 (2000): 2036.

Lebow, M. A., and A. Chen. "Overshadowed by the Amygdala: The Bed Nucleus of the Stria Terminalis Emerges as Key to Psychiatric Disorders." *Molecular Psychiatry* 21 (2016): 450–63.

Mansouri, A., K. Kosidou, and I. Savic. "Anatomical and Functional Findings in Female-to-Male Transsexuals: Testing a New Hypothesis." *Cerebral Cortex* 27, no. 2 (2017): 998–1010.

Pol, Hilleke E. Hulshoff, Peggy T. Cohen-Kettenis, Neeltje E. M. Van Haren, Jiska S. Peper, Rachel G. H. Brans, Wiepke Cahn, Hugo G. Schnack, Louis J. G. Gooren, and Rene S. Kahn. "Changing Your Sex Changes Your Brain: Influences of Testosterone and Estrogen on Adult Human Brain Structure." *European Journal of Endocrinology* 144 (November 1, 2006): 107–14.

Rametti, Giuseppina, Beatriz Carrillo, Esther Gómez-Gil,
     Carme Junque, Leire Zubiarre-Elorza, Santiago
     Segovia, Ángel Gomez, and Antonio Guillamon. "The
     Microstructure of White Matter in Male to Female
     Transsexuals Before Cross-Sex Hormonal Treatment: A
     DTI Study." *Journal of Psychiatric Research* 45, no. 7 (July
     2011): 949–54.

Rametti, Giuseppina, Beatriz Carrillo, Esther Gómez-Gil,
     Carme Junque, Santiago Segovia, Angel Manuel Gómez,
     and Antonio Guillamón. "White Matter Microstructure
     in Female to Male Transsexuals before Cross-Sex
     Hormonal Treatment: A Diffusion Tensor Imaging
     Study." *Journal of Psychiatric Research* 45, no. 2 (2011):
     199–204.

Ruigrok, Amber N. V., Gholamreza Salimi-Khorshidi, Meng-
     Chuan Lai, Simon Baron-Cohena, Michael V. Lombardo,
     Roger J. Taitf, and John Suckling. "A Meta-analysis
     of Sex Differences in Human Brain Structure."
     Neuroscience and Behavioral Reviews 39 (2014): 34–50.

Staphorsius, Annemeike S., Baudewijntje P. C. Kreukels,
     Peggy T. Cohen-Kettenis, Dick J. Veltmanc, Sarah M.
     Burkea, Sebastian E. E. Schagend, Femke M. Wouters,
     Henriëtte A. Delemarre-van de Waal, and Julie Bakker.
     "Puberty Suppression and Executive Functioning: An
     fMRI-Study in Adolescents with Gender Dysphoria."
     Psychoneuroendocrinology 56 (June 2015): 190–99.

Swaab, Dick F., and Alicia Garcia-Falgueras. "Sexual
     Differentiation of the Human Brain in Relation to
     Gender Identity and Sexual Orientation." *Functional
     Neurology* 24, no. 1 (2009): 17–28.

Zhou, Jiang-Ning, Michel A. Hofman, Louis J. G. Gooren,
     and Dick F. Swaab. "A Sex Difference in the Human

Brain and Its Relation to Transsexuality." *Nature* 378 (November 1995): 68–70.

GENDER REASSIGNMENT SURGERY

Colebunders, Britt, Salvatore D'Arpa, Steven Weigers, Nicolaas Lumen, Piet Hoebeke, and Stan Monstrey. "Female-to Male Gender Reassignment Surgery." In *Principles of Transgender Medicine and Surgery*, edited by Randi Ettner, Stan Monstrey, and Eli Coleman, 297–317. 2nd ed. New York: Routledge, 2016.

Colebunders, Britt, Sam Brondeel, Salvatore D'Arpa, Piet Hoebeke, and Stan Monstrey. "An Update on the Surgical Treatment of Transgender Patients." *Sexual Medicine Reviews* 5 (2017): 103–9.

Colebunders, Britt, Wim Verhaeghe, Katrien Bonte, Salvatore D'Arpa, and Stan Monstrey. "Male-to-Female Gender Reassignment Surgery." In *Principles of Transgender Medicine and Surgery*, edited by Randi Ettner, Stan Monstrey, and Eli Coleman, 250–78. 2nd ed. New York: Routledge, 2016.

Dhejne, Cecilia, Paul Lichtenstein, Marcus Boman, Anna L. V. Johansson, Niklas Langström, and Mikael Landen. "Long-Term Follow-Up of Transsexual Persons Undergoing Sex-Reassignment Surgery: Cohort Study in Sweden." *PloS One* 6, no. 2 (February 2011): 1–8.

Fitzgibbons, Richard, Philip M. Sutton, and Dale O'Leary. "The Psychopathology of 'Sex Reassignment' Surgery: Assessing Its Medical, Psychological, and Ethical Appropriateness." *National Catholic Bioethics Center* (2009): 97–125.

Golpanian, Samuel, Kenneth A. Guier, Ling Tao, Priscila G. Sanchez, Klara Sputova, and Christopher J. Salgado.

"Phalloplasty and Urethral (Re)construction: A Chronological Timeline." *Anaplastology* 5, no. 2 (2016): 1–8.

Jordjevic, Miroslav L., Marta R. Bizic, Dragana Duisin, Mark-Bram Bouman, and Marlon Buncamper. "Reversal Surgery in Regretful Male-to-Female Transsexuals after Sex Reassignment Surgery." *Journal of Sexual Medicine* 13, no. 6 (2016): 1000–1007.

Kline, Craig, and David Schrock. "What Is Gender Reassignment Surgery? A Medical Assessment with a Biblical Appraisal." *Journal of Biblical Manhood and Womanhood* 20, no. 1 (2015): 35–47.

Krege, S., A. Bex, and G. Lummen. "Male-to-Female Transsexualism: A Technique, Results, and Long-Term Follow Up in 66 Patients." *British Journal of Urology* 88 (2001): 396–402.

Rashid, Mamoon, and Muhammad Sarmad Tamiimy. "Phalloplasty: The Dream and the Reality." *Indian Journal of Plastic Surgery* 46, no. 2 (2013): 283–93.

Schaff, Juergen, and Nikolaos A. Papadopulos. "A New Protocol for Complete Phalloplasty with Free Sensate and Prelaminated Osteofasciocutaneous Flaps: Experience in 37 Patients." *Microsurgery* 29, no. 5 (2009): 413–19.

Selvaggi, Gennaro, and James Bellringer. "Gender Reassignment Surgery: An Overview." *Nature Review of Urology* 8, no. 5 (2011): 274–82.

Selvaggi, Gennaro, Peter Ceulemans, Griet De Cuypere, Koen VanLanduyt, Phillip Blondeel, Moustapha Hamdi, Cameron Bowman, and Stan Monstrey. "Gender Identity Disorder: General Overview and Surgical Treatment for Vaginoplasty in Male-to-Female

Transsexuals." *Plastic and Reconstructive Surgery* 116, no. 6 (2005): 135–45.

Sohn, M. H., M. Hatzinger, and K. Wirsam. "Genital Reassignment Surgery in Male-to-Female Transsexuals: Do We Have Guidelines or Standards?" *Handchirurgie Mikrochirurgie Plastiche Chirurgie* 45, no. 4 (2013): 207–10.

Sutcliffe, P. A., S. Dixon, R. L. Akehurst, A. Wilkinson, A. Shippam, S. White, R. Richards, and C. M. Caddy. "Evaluation of Surgical Procedures for Sex Reassignment: A Systematic Review." *Journal of Plastic, Reconstructive, and Aesthetic Surgery* 62, no. 3 (2009): 294–306.

Wangjiraniran, Burin, Gennaro Selvaggi, Prayuth Chokrungvaranont, Sirachai Jindarak, Sutin Khobunsongserm, and Preecha Tiewtranon. "Male-to-Female Vaginoplasty: Preecha's Surgical Technique." *Journal of Plastic Surgery and Hand Surgery* 49, no. 3 (2015): 153–59.

GENETIC RESEARCH

Bentz, E. K., C. Schneeberger, L. A. Hefler, M. van Trotsenburg, U. Kaufmann, J. C. Huber, and C. B. Tempfer. "A Common Polymorphism Of the SRD5A2 Gene and Transsexualism." *Reproductive Sciences* 14, no. 7 (2007): 705– 9.

Bentz, E. K., L. A. Hefler, U. Kaufmann, J. C. Huber, A. Kolbus, and C. B. Tempfer. "A Polymorphism of the CYP17 Gene Related to Sex Steroid Metabolism Is Associated with Female-to-Male but Not Male-to-Male Transsexualism." *Fertility and Sterility* 90, no. 1 (2008): 56–59.

Diamond, Milton. "Transsexuality among Twins; Identity Concordance, Transition, Rearing, and Orientation." *International Journal of Transgenderism* 14, no. 1 (2013): 24–38.

Fernandez, R., J. Cortés-Cortés, I. Esteva, E. Gomez-Gil, M. C. Almaraz, E. Lema, Teresa Rumbo, J. J. Haro-Mora, E. Roda, Antonio Guillamón, and E. Pásaro. "The CYP17 MspA1 Polymorphism and Gender Dysphoria." *Journal of Sexual Medicine* 12, no. 6 (2015): 1329–33.

Fernandez, Rose, Isabel Esteva, Esther Gomez-Gil, Teresa Rumbo, Mari Cruz Almaraz, Ester Roda, Juan-Jesús Haro-Mora, Antonio Guillamón, and Eduardo Pásaro. "The (CA)n Polymorphism of *ER*" Gene Is Associated with FtM Transsexualism." *Journal of Sexual Medicine* 11, no. 3 (2014): 720–28.

Gao, Wenqing, Casey E. Bohl, and James T. Dalton. "Chemistry and Structural Biology of Androgen Receptor." *Chemical Reviews* 105, no. 9 (2005): 3352–70.

Hare, Lauren, Pascal Bernard, Francisco J. Sánchez, Paul N. Baird, Eric Vilain, Trudy Kennedy, and Vincent R. Harley. "Androgen Receptor Repeat Length Polymorphism Associated with Male-to-Female Transsexualism." *Biological Psychiatry* 65, no. 1 (2009): 93–96.

Henningsson, Susanne, Lars Westberg, Staffan Nilsson, Bengt Lundström, Lisa Ekselius, Owe Bodlund, Eva Lindström, Monika Hellstrand, Roland Rosmond, Elias Eriksson, and Mikael Landen. "Sex Steroid-Related Genes and Male-to-Female Transsexualism." *Psychoneuroendocrinology* 30 (2005): 657–64.

Heylens, Gunter, Griet De Cuypere, Kenneth J. Zucker, Cleo Schelfaut, Els Elaut, Heidi Vanden Bossche, Elfride De

Baere, and Guy T'Sjoen. "Gender Identity Disorder in Twins: A Review of the Case Report Literature." *Journal of Sexual Medicine* 9, no. 3 (2012): 751–57.

Klink, Daniel, and Martin Den Heijer. "Genetic Aspects of Gender Identity Development and Gender Dysphoria." In *Gender Dysphoria and Disorders of Sexual Development: Progress in Care and Knowledge*, edited by Baudewijntje P. C. Kreukels, Thomas D. Steensma, and Annelou L. C. de Vries, 25–51. New York: Springer, 2014.

Krishnan, R. Harish, Amul J. Sakharkar, Tara L. Teppen, Tiffani D. M. Berkel, and Subhash C. Pandey. "The Epigenetic Landscape of Alcoholism." *International Review of Neurobiology* 115 (2014): 75–116.

Ujike, H., K. Otani, M., Nakatsuka, K. Ishii, A. Sasaki, T. Oishi, T. Sato, Y. Okahisa, Y. Matsumoto, Y. Namba, Y. Kimata, and S. Kuroda. "Association Study of Gender Identity Disorder and Sex-Hormone Related Genes." *Progress in Neuro-Psychopharmacology and Biological Psychiatry* 33, no. 7 (2009): 1241–44.

HORMONE THERAPY

Asschemann, H., E. J. Giltay, J. A. Megens, W. P. de Ronde, M. A. van Trotsenburg, and L. J. Gooren. "A Long-Term Follow-Up Study of Mortality in Transsexuals Receiving Treatment with Cross-Sex Hormones." *European Journal of Endocrinology* 164, no. 4 (2011): 635–42.

Cohen-Kettenis, P. T., and S. H. van Goozen. "Pubertal Delay as an Aid in Diagnosis and Treatment of a Transsexual Adolescent." *European Child and Adolescent Psychiatry* 7, no. 4 (1998): 246–48.

Dahl, Marshall, Jamie L. Feldman, Joshua M. Goldberg, and Afshin Jaberi. "Physical Aspects of Transgender

Endocrine Therapy." *International Journal of Transgenderism* 9, nos. 3–4 (2006): 111–34.

Delemarre-van de Waal, Henriette A., and Peggy T. Cohen-Kettenis. "Clinical Management of Gender Identity Disorder in Adolescents: A Protocol on Psychological and Paediatric Endocrinology." *European Journal of Endocrinology* 155 (2006): S131–S137.

Dizon, D. S., T. Tejada-Berges, S. Koelliker, M. Steinhoff, and C. O. Granai. "Ovarian Cancer Associated with Testosterone Supplementation in a Female-to-Male Transsexual Patient." *Gynecologic and Obstetric Investigation* 62, no. 4 (2006): 226–28.

Hembree, Wylie, Peggy Cohen-Kettenis, Henriette A. Delemarre-van de Waal, Louis J. Gooren, Walter J. Meyer III, Norman P. Spack, Vin Tangpricha, and Victor M. Montori. "Endocrine Treatment of Transsexual Persons: An Endocrine Society Clinical Practice Guideline." *Journal of Clinical Endocrinology and Metabolism* 94, no. 9 (2009): 3132–54.

Hruz, Paul W., Lawrence S. Mayer, and Paul R. McHugh. "Growing Pains: Problems with Puberty Suppression in Treating Gender Dysphoria." *The New Atlantis* 52 (Spring 2017): 3–36.

Kesteren, P. J. van, H. Asscheman, J. A. Megens, and L. J. Gooren. "Mortality and Morbidity in Transsexual Subjects Treated with Cross-Sex Hormones." *Clinical Endocrinology* 47, no. 3 (September 1997): 337–42.

Meyer-Bahlburg, Heino F. L. "Sex Steroids and Variants of Gender Identity." In *Endocrine and Neuropsychiatric Disorders*, edited by Eliza B. Greer, 435–52. Philadelphia: Elsevier, 2013.

Murad, M. H., M. B. Elamin, M. Z. Garcia, R. J. Mullan, A. Murad, P. J. Erwin, and V. M. Montori. "Hormonal Therapy and Sex Reassignment: A Systematic Review and Meta-analysis of Quality of Life and Psychosocial Outcomes." *Clinical Endocrinology* 72, no. 2 (2010): 214–31.

Weinand, Jamie D., and Joshua D. Safer. "Hormone Therapy in Transgender Adults Is Safe with Provider Supervision: A Review of Hormone Therapy Sequelae for Transgender Individuals." *Journal of Clinical and Translational Endocrinology* 2, no. 2 (2015): 55–60.

Wierckx, K., F. Elaut, E. Declercq, G. Heylens, G. De Cuypere, Y. Taes, J. M. Kaufman, and G. T. Sjoen. "Prevalence of Cardiovascular Disease and Cancer During Cross-Sex Hormone Therapy in a Large Cohort of Trans Persons: A Case-Control Study." *European Journal of Endocrinology* 169 (2013): 471–78.

Wylie, Kevan Richard, Robert Fung, Claudia Boshier, and Margaret Rotchell. "Recommendations of Endocrine Treatment for Patients with Gender Dysphoria." *Sexual and Relationship Therapy* 24, no. 2 (May 2009): 175–87.

Zubiaurre-Elorza, L., C. Junque, E. Gómez-Gil, A. Guillamon. "Effects of Cross-Sex Hormone Treatment on Cortical Thickness in Transsexual Individuals." *Journal of Sexual Medicine* 11, no. 5 (2014): 1248–61.

BIBLICAL, THEOLOGICAL, AND HISTORICAL SOURCES

Baxter. Richard. *The Reformed Pastor.* Edited by William Brown. Edinburgh: Banner of Truth Trust, 2012.

Block, Daniel I. *Deuteronomy.* NIV Application Commentary. Grand Rapids: Zondervan, 2012.

Cairns, Ian. *Deuteronomy: Word and Presence.* International Theological Commentary. Grand Rapids: Eerdmans, 1992.

Calvin, John. *A Commentary on Genesis.* Translated by John King. Edinburgh: Banner of Truth Trust, 1965.

Dalley, Stephanie, trans. "Erra and Ishum." In *The Context of Scripture*, edited by William W. Hallo, 1:404–16. Leiden: Brill, 1997.

Danker, Frederick W., Walter Bauer, William F. Arndt, and F. Wilbur Gingrich, eds. *A Greek-English Lexicon of the New Testament and Other Early Christian Literature.* 3rd ed. Chicago: University of Chicago Press, 2000.

Edwards, Jonathan. *The Works of Jonathan Edwards.* Vol. 2, *A Treatise concerning Religious Affections.* Edited by John E. Smith. New Haven, CT: Yale University Press, 1959.

Erickson, Millard. *Christian Theology.* 2nd ed. Grand Rapids: Baker, 1998.

Feinberg, Charles L. *Jeremiah.* Expositor's Bible Commentary 6. Grand Rapids: Zondervan, 1986.

Fox, Nili Sacher. "Gender Transformation and Transgression: Contextualizing the Prohibition of Cross-Dressing in Deuteronomy 22:5." In *Mishneh Todah: Studies in Deuteronomy and Its Cultural Context in Honor of Jeffrey H. Tigay*, edited by Nili Sacher Fox, D. A. Glat-Gilad, and M. J. Williams, 49–71. Winona Lake, IN: Eisenbrauns, 2009.

Gagnon, Robert. *The Bible and Homosexual Practice.* Nashville: Abingdon, 2001.

Garland, David E. *Colossians and Philemon.* NIV Application Commentary. Grand Rapids: Zondervan, 1998.

Gasparro, Giulia Sfameni. *Soteriology and Mystic Aspects in the Cult of Cybele and Attis.* Leiden: Brill, 1985.

Grisanti, Michael A. "t'b." In *New International Dictionary of Old Testament Theology and Exegesis*, edited by Willem A. VanGemeren, 4:314-18. Grand Rapids: Zondervan, 1997.

Grudem, Wayne. *Systematic Theology*. Grand Rapids: Zondervan, 1994.

Hamilton, Victor. *The Book of Genesis Chapters 1-17*. New International Old Testament Commentary. Grand Rapids: Eerdmans, 1990.

Kaiser, Walter. *Toward Old Testament Ethics*. Grand Rapids: Zondervan, 1991.

———. "*Min*, Kind." In *Theological Wordbook of the Old Testament*, edited by R. Laird Harris, Gleason Archer, and Bruce Waltke, 1:503-4. Chicago: Moody Press, 1980.

Mare, W. Harold. *1 Corinthians*. Expositor's Bible Commentary 10. Grand Rapids: Zondervan, 1976.

Merrill, Eugene H. *Deuteronomy*. New American Commentary. Nashville: Broadman & Holman, 1994.

Moseley, N. Allan. *Thinking against the Grain: Developing a Biblical Worldview in a Culture of Myths*. Grand Rapids: Kregel, 2003.

Nash, Ronald. *Life's Ultimate Questions: An Introduction to Philosophy*. Grand Rapids: Zondervan, 1999.

Nolland, John. *The Gospel of Matthew*. New International Greek Testament Commentary. Grand Rapids: Eerdmans, 2005.

Patterson, Paige. *The Troubled Triumphant Church: An Exposition of First Corinthians*. Dallas: Criswell, 1983.

Roberts, Vaughn. *Transgender: A Talking Points Book*. Purcellville, VA: The Good Book Company, 2016.

Rogers, Nigel. *The Roman Empire*. New York: Metro Books, 2008.

Roscoe, Will. "Priests of the Goddess: Gender Transgression in Ancient Religion." *History of Religions* 35, no. 3 (1996): 195-230.

Ross, Allen P. *Creation and Blessing: A Guide to the Study and Exposition of Genesis*. Grand Rapids: Baker, 1998.

Thiselton, Anthony C. *The First Epistle to the Corinthians*. New International Greek Testament Commentary. Grand Rapids: Eerdmans, 2000.

Turcan, Robert. *The Cults of the Roman Empire*. Malden, MA: Blackwell, 1992.

Vermaseren, Maarten J. *Cybele and Attis: The Myth and the Cult*. Translated by A. M. H. Lemmers. London: Thames and Hudson, 1977.

SUBJECT INDEX

BIBLICAL REFERENCES